EXCEL 5

HOW TO WORK WITH
Lists
Pivot tables &
External databases

For Windows

Anne Prince

Mike Murach & Associates

4697 West Jacquelyn Avenue, Fresno, California 93722-6427
(209) 275-3335

| Managing editor: | Mike Murach |
| Graphics designer: | Steve Ehlers |

Other books for Windows users	The Least You Need to Know about Windows 3.1
	Work Like a Pro with Excel 5 for Windows
	Work Like a Pro with Word 6 for Windows
	The Essential Guide: Excel 5.0 for Windows
	The Essential Guide: Word 6.0 for Windows
	The Essential Guide: 1-2-3 for Windows Release 4
	The Essential Guide: WordPerfect 6.0 for Windows
	Word 6 for Windows: How to use the Mail Merge feature

Books for DOS users	The Essential Guide: WordPerfect 6.0 for DOS
	The Least You Need to Know about DOS, Second Edition
	The Only DOS Book You'll Ever Need, Second Edition
	The Least You Need to Know about Lotus 1-2-3 (releases 2.0 through 3.1)
	The Practical Guide to Lotus 1-2-3 (releases 2.0 through 3.4)
	The Least You Need to Know about WordPerfect 5.0 and 5.1
	DOS, WordPerfect, and Lotus Essentials

ISBN: 0-911625-87-9

Library of Congress Cataloging-in-Publication Data
Prince, Anne.
    Excel 5 for Windows : how to work with lists, pivot tables &
external databases / Anne Prince.
        p.   cm.
    Includes index.
    ISBN 0-911625-87-9 (paperback)
    1. Microsoft Excel for Windows. 2. Business--Computer programs.
3. Electronic spreadsheets. I. Title. II. Title: How to work with
lists, pivot tables & external databases.
    HF5548.4.M523P753   1995
    005.369--dc20   95-7064
                                                                      CIP

Contents

Introduction   V

Chapter 1   How to set up a list and use filters and forms   1

Chapter 2   How to sort and summarize the data in a list   13

Chapter 3   How to use pivot tables   21

Chapter 4   How to use Microsoft Query to import data from an   37
             external database

Index   61

Introduction

Most books on Excel 5 focus on its spreadsheet and charting capabilities. But Excel 5 also has a rich set of features for working with data that's organized in lists or databases. These features are particularly useful when you use them to work with data that's created and maintained by another program like *Oracle* or *Access*. Then, you can download portions of the database into Excel and use Excel to work with that data.

Because the list and database features are relatively complicated, these features can be hard to master on your own. That's why we wrote this book. Its only prerequisite is that you know how to use Excel 5 to create simple spreadsheets. If you can do that, this book will help you master the list and database features as quickly and easily as possible.

To start, chapter 1 shows you how to set up a list in Excel. You can think of a list as a simple database. It also shows you how to use filters and forms to manipulate the data in a list. Then, chapter 2 shows you how to sort a list and how to create subtotals for the data in a list. And chapter 3 shows you how to use pivot tables with a list. Pivot tables, which are a new feature of Excel 5, let you cross tabulate the data in a list to get different perspectives on it.

The fourth and last chapter in this book is perhaps the most valuable one. It shows you how to use *Microsoft Query* to retrieve or extract data from a database that's created by another program. Although *Query* is a separate program, it comes with Excel, and the two are tightly integrated. After you use *Query* to import the fields and records of an external database into an Excel list, you can use the Excel techniques that you learned in the first three chapters to work with the list. If you're going to be working mostly with external databases, you may want to read this chapter of the book first.

To make this book as effective as possible, we've used some presentation methods that you won't find in other books or training materials. Most important, all of the required information is presented in the illustrations (figures) so you don't have to dig through the text to find it. Then, to make the book easier to read, each figure and its related text are presented on the same page. These presentation methods not only help you learn more quickly on your first reading of the book, but they also make this the ideal reference book later on.

Because you learn more by doing than by reading, exercises are included at strategic points in each chapter. In chapter 1, for example, the first exercise has you create your own list in Excel. Then, the rest of the exercises in that chapter and in the next two chapters have you use that list to experiment with the features you'll learn in those chapters. In the last chapter, the first exercise has you create a dBase file from the Excel list. Then, the rest of the exercises have you use that file to experiment with the features for importing data from an external database.

If you have any comments about this book, we would enjoy hearing from you. That's why there's a postage-paid form at the back of this book. In particular, we would like to know whether you've found our presentation methods more effective than others that you've used. With your help, we can continue to improve our books so they help you get the most from your software, as quickly and easily as possible.

Chapter 1

How to set up a list and use filters and forms

A *list* is a range of rows in a worksheet that contain similar data and have labeled columns. You can think of a list as a simple database where each row is a record and each column is a field. In this chapter, you'll learn how to set up a list, how to select records from a list, and how to use a data form to maintain the data in a list.

Although you can set up a list in Excel using the techniques presented in this chapter, you can also create a list by importing data from an external database. You'll learn how to do that in chapter 4. Whether you set up your own list or create one from an external database, you can use the features presented in this chapter and the next two chapters to work with the data.

How to set up a list

How to use the AutoFilter feature to select records from a list
    How to find selected records
    How to specify custom selection criteria
    How to remove filtering from a list

How to use the Advanced Filter feature to select records from a list
    How to set up a criteria range
    How to find selected records
    How to create a results table

How to use a data form to work with the data in a list
    How to browse, delete, change, and add records to a list
    How to select the records displayed in the data form

Perspective

Summary

How to set up a list

Figure 1-1 shows you how to set up a list. Here, you can see that the first row in a list, called the *header row*, contains a series of *column labels*, or *field names*, one for each column in the list. Each row below the header row represents one *record* in the list. And each cell in a record represents a *field*.

To create a list like this one, you start by entering the column labels. You should enter the column labels without any columns separating them, and each column label must occupy only one cell. Although the column labels in figure 1-1 start in cell A1, you can start a list anywhere in a worksheet.

Next, you enter the records of the list directly under the column labels. You should enter these records with no empty rows separating them. If you need to add records later, you can do that by inserting a row or by using the data form feature presented later in this chapter.

Finally, you format the list. In figure 1-1, for example, the column widths were changed to accommodate the data and the numeric columns were right-aligned. In addition, the header row was boldfaced and underlined.

Once the list is set up the way you want it, you can use several of the commands in the Data menu to work with it. In this chapter, I'll show you how to use the Form and Filter commands. In addition to these commands, you can use many other commands to maintain the list. For example, you can use the Rows command in the Insert menu to insert rows, and you can use the Delete command in the Edit menu to delete rows.

Procedure

1. Enter column labels (field names) in a single row to name the fields in the list.

2. Enter the data for the items in the list (records) in the rows directly below the column labels.

3. Format the list so it is easy to work with.

The Employee list

	A	B	C	D	E	F	G
1	Last name	First name	Dept.	Job code	Age	Current salary	
2	Smith	Mary	Admin	1	23	$24,600	
3	Jones	Georgia	Mktg	3	43	$47,500	
4	Long	John	Prod	3	52	$39,900	
5	Johnson	Edward	Admin	2	30	$33,250	
6	Jones	John	Prod	2	33	$31,400	
7	Williams	Alice	Admin	1	50	$28,900	
8	Allen	Joel	Admin	2	25	$30,000	
9	Clay	Kurt	Mktg	2	43	$41,250	
10	Burkes	Patricia	Prod	1	52	$28,500	
11	Andrews	Anne	Admin	3	30	$34,000	
12	Russell	Barry	Prod	2	33	$31,500	
13	Thompson	John	Mktg	1	50	$26,500	
14							

Header row (column labels)

Records

Note

• If a column label is wider than the column like "Job code" in the example above, use the Wrap Text option in the Alignment tab of the Format dialog box to continue the label on the next line in the same cell.

Figure 1-1   How to set up a list

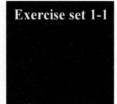**Exercise set 1-1**   1. Use the procedure and data in figure 1-1 to set up the Employee list. Be sure to adjust the column widths and cell alignments so they're appropriate for the data, and format the header row so it stands out from the data. Save the list using the file name EMPLOYEE.

How to use the AutoFilter feature to select records from a list

A major enhancement to version 5 of Excel is the AutoFilter feature. With this feature, you can display the records in a list that meet the criteria you specify by applying a *filter* to the list. Then, all the records in the list that don't meet the criteria are hidden from view, or filtered.

How to find selected records

Figure 1-2 shows you how to use the AutoFilter feature to display selected records in a list. As you can see, you can use this feature to filter a list based on the values in one or more columns. You can also use the All, Custom, Blanks and NonBlanks options that appear in the list for each column to remove filtering from a column, specify custom selection criteria, display all the rows that don't have data in the column, or display all the rows that have data in the column. You'll learn more about the All and Custom options later in this chapter.

Although you'll usually use the mouse techniques described in figure 1-2 to apply AutoFilter criteria to a list, you can also use the keyboard techniques shown in figure 1-3. In particular, you'll want to use the last technique for highlighting a value in a drop-down list if the list contains many values. Then, you can move to the first value in the list that begins with the character you type.

Procedure

1. Place the cell pointer on any cell in the list and select the AutoFilter command from the Filter submenu of the Data menu. Then, Excel adds drop-down arrows to each cell in the header row.

2. Click on the drop-down arrow for a column to access a list of the values in that column:

3. Select one of the values in the list, and Excel hides all the rows that don't match that value:

4. Repeat steps 2 and 3 for each column you want to base the selection on.

Figure 1-2   How to use the AutoFilter feature to find selected records

Procedure

1. Move the cell pointer to the column label for the column you want to filter and type Alt+Down-arrow. Then, Excel displays the drop-down list for that column.

2. Move the highlight to the value or option you want to base the selection on using the keys listed below and press the Enter key.

Keys you can use to highlight an item

Up-arrow or Down-arrow	Move up or down one item.
Home or End	Move to the top or bottom of the list.
Page-Up or Page-Down	Move up or down the height of the list box.
character	Move to the first value in the list that starts with *character*.

Figure 1-3   How to use the keyboard to select AutoFilter criteria

How to specify custom selection criteria

When you select a value from an AutoFilter drop-down list, Excel finds records that contain that value. In other words, Excel uses the "equals" relational operator. If you need to select records based on other relational conditions, you can select the Custom option. Then, you can specify custom selection criteria as illustrated in figure 1-4.

From the Custom AutoFilter dialog box, you can select from several relational conditions in addition to the "equals" condition. You can also specify comparison values that aren't present in the selected column. Finally, you can specify two comparison criteria. If you do, you must also select one of the logical operators: And or Or.

Procedure

1. Enable the AutoFilter feature for a list, and click on the drop-down arrow for the column you want to base the selection on.

2. Select the Custom option from the drop-down list and this dialog box appears:

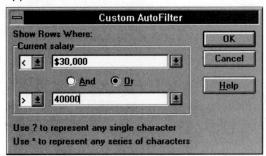

3. Specify one or two comparison criteria for the column by selecting a relational operator and selecting or entering a comparison value for each. If the comparison value is a text string, it can include the question mark (?) and asterisk (*) wildcard characters. If you specify two criteria, choose a logical operator (And or Or).

4. Click on the OK button and Excel filters the list:

	A	B	C	D	E	F	G
1	Last name	First name	Dept.	Job code	A	Current sala	
2	Smith	Mary	Admin	1	23	$24,600	
3	Jones	Georgia	Mktg	3	43	$47,500	
7	Williams	Alice	Admin	1	50	$28,900	
9	Clay	Kurt	Mktg	2	43	$41,250	
10	Burkes	Patricia	Prod	1	52	$28,500	
13	Thompson	John	Mktg	1	50	$26,500	
14							

Figure 1-4   How to use the AutoFilter feature to specify custom selection criteria

How to remove filtering from a list

Figure 1-5 shows you three ways to remove filtering from a list. As you can see, you can remove the filtering from a single column or from the entire list. You can also remove the AutoFilter arrows when you remove all the filtering. You might want to do that when you're done working with the list.

How to remove the filtering based on a single column
Select the All filter option from the drop-down list for the column.

How to remove all the filtering from a list
Select the Show All command from the Filter submenu of the Data menu.

How to remove all the filtering and the AutoFilter arrows
Select the AutoFilter command from the Filter submenu of the Data menu.

Figure 1-5   How to remove filtering from a list

**Exercise set 1-2**

1. Use the procedure in figure 1-2 to display the records for employees in the Mktg department with job code 2. When you're done, remove the filtering from the list using one of the techniques in figure 1-5.

2. Use the procedure in figure 1-4 to display the records for employees who are 30 or older. Then, modify the criteria so that only records for employees between the ages of 30 and 50 are displayed. When you're done, remove the filtering from the list.

3. Use the procedure in figure 1-4 to display the records for employees whose last names start with one of the letters from J to Z. Then, modify the criteria and use a wildcard to display the records for employees whose last names start with the letter J. When you're done, remove the filtering from the list.

How to use the Advanced Filter feature to select records from a list

When you filter a list by selecting criteria from two or more columns using the AutoFilter feature, the condition in each column must be met for a record to be displayed. In other words, the implied logical operator between the condition in each column is And. If you want to select records based on the values in one column *or* another column, you have to use the Advanced Filter feature. Before you can use this feature, though, you have to set up a criteria range. Then, you can use the Advanced Filter feature to filter the records in a list or to create a results table.

How to set up a criteria range

Figure 1-6 shows you how to set up a criteria range. A criteria range consists of one or more column labels from the list you're filtering and one or more conditions for each column. If you enter the conditions for two columns in the same row, both of the conditions must be true for the criteria to be satisfied. If you enter the conditions in different rows, either one or the other of the conditions must be true. The criteria in figure 1-6, for example, will select records for employees who work in the Admin department and have a salary of $30,000 or more *or* for employees who work in the Mktg department and have a salary of $40,000 or more.

Procedure

1. Enter the column label of each column you want to specify criteria for in a single row.

2. Enter one or more comparison conditions for each column in the rows immediately below the labels. To indicate a logical And operation between two or more conditions, enter the conditions in the same row. To indicate a logical Or operation between two or more conditions, enter the conditions in different rows.

A criteria range that specifies conditions for two columns in the Employee list

	Dept.	Current salary	
15			
16	Admin	>=30000	
17	Mktg	>=40000	
18			

Notes

- You can omit the relational operator from an equals condition, as illustrated in the conditions for the Dept. column above.

- If you specify a text string in a comparison condition, enclose it in quotation marks if you want Excel to look for an exact match. Otherwise, any values that begin with the characters will meet the condition. You can also use the asterisk (*) and question mark wildcards (?) in a text string.

- If you want two conditions for the same column to be satisfied, enter the column label twice and enter a condition in the same row in each column.

- You can also use computed criteria in a criteria range. To do that, enter a label other than a column label, and enter a logical formula (one that evaluates to true or false) for the condition. The formula must refer to at least one column in the list and may refer to cells outside the list. For more information on using computed criteria, see the online help for setting up criteria ranges.

Figure 1-6   How to set up a criteria range

How to find selected records

The most difficult part of using the Advanced Filter feature is setting up the criteria range. Once you do that, you can use the procedure in figure 1-7 to filter the list based on the criteria in the criteria range. Note that each time you filter a list with the Advanced Filter feature, the filter replaces any existing filter. So you can't use this feature to perform successive filter operations as you can with the AutoFilter feature.

Access   **Menu**   Data ➡ Filter ➡ Advanced Filter

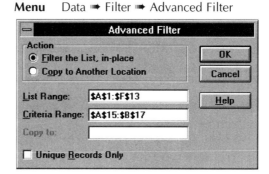

Procedure

1. Place the cell pointer on a cell in the list and access the Advanced Filter dialog box.

2. Enter the range that contains the criteria (including the labels) by typing it in or by clicking in the Criteria Range text box and selecting the range.

3. Click on the OK button and Excel filters the list:

	A	B	C	D	E	F	G
1	Last name	First name	Dept.	Job code	Age	Current salary	
3	Jones	Georgia	Mktg	3	43	$47,500	
5	Johnson	Edward	Admin	2	30	$33,250	
8	Allen	Joel	Admin	2	25	$30,000	
9	Clay	Kurt	Mktg	2	43	$41,250	
11	Andrews	Anne	Admin	3	30	$34,000	
14							
15	Dept.	Current salary					
16	Admin	>=30000					
17	Mktg	>=40000					
18							

Notes

- If you select the Unique Records Only option, Excel hides duplicate records. You can select this option with or without selecting criteria.

- To redisplay hidden rows, select the Show All command from the Filter submenu of the Data menu.

Figure 1-7   How to use the Advanced Filter feature to find selected records

How to create a results table

Instead of hiding the rows in a list that don't satisfy the criteria you specify, you can create a *results table*. A results table is a list that's separate from the original list and that contains only the records that satisfy the criteria. The procedure for creating a results table is presented in figure 1-8. As you can see, this procedure is similar to the procedure for filtering a list using the Advanced Filter feature. The only differences are that you select the Copy To Another Location option in the dialog box and you specify where you want to place the results table.

A results table created by the Advanced Filter command is similar to what some other spreadsheet programs (like *Lotus 1-2-3*) call a *query table*. When you create a query table, however, you can select not only the records you want to include, but the fields as well. The only way to do that with an Excel list is to create a results table, then delete the fields you don't want. Note that when you make changes to a results table, the original list is unaffected.

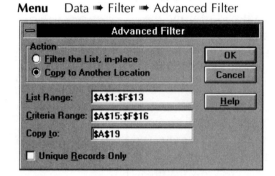

Access   **Menu**   Data ➡ Filter ➡ Advanced Filter

Procedure

1. Place the cell pointer on a cell in the list.

2. Access the Advanced Filter dialog box, and select the Copy To Another Location option.

3. Enter the criteria range in the Criteria Range text box, and specify the location for the results table by entering a reference for the cell in the upper left corner of the range in the Copy To text box.

4. Click on the OK button, and the filtered list is copied to the specified location.

Notes

- You can also enter a range in the Copy To text box. If you do, the range must include the same number of columns as the list. If all of the records that meet the criteria don't fit in the range, Excel asks if you want to paste the remaining rows.

- Excel doesn't let you specify a Copy To location outside of the current worksheet. However, it does let you specify a List Range and a Criteria Range in another worksheet. So if you want to create a results table in another worksheet, issue the Advanced Filter command from that worksheet.

Figure 1-8   How to use the Advanced Filter feature to create a results table

Exercise set 1-3

1. Use the procedure in figure 1-6 to set up a criteria range that will display the records for employees with job code 2 whose salary is over 30,000 or employees with job code 3 whose salary is over 35,000. Then, use the procedure in figure 1-7 to filter the list using the criteria range. When you're done, use the Show All command in the Filter submenu of the Data menu to remove the filtering from the list.

2. Use the procedure in figure 1-8 to create a results table from the Employee list using the criteria range you created in exercise 1.

How to use a data form to work with the data in a list

Excel's Form command lets you access a special dialog box called a *data form* to retrieve, edit, add, and delete the records in a list. When you issue this command, Excel builds the data form so it contains a text box for each field in the list that can be modified. In effect, the data form is a data entry and inquiry panel for the list.

How to browse, delete, change, and add records to a list

Figure 1-9 shows you how to use a data form to browse, delete, change, and add records to a list. As you can see, the data form displays one record at a time. When a record is displayed, you can delete or modify it. To add a new record, you have to display a blank data form.

When you delete a record from a list using a data form, you should know that Excel does not delete the row it occupies. Instead, it moves any records that follow the deleted record up to fill the empty row. Likewise, when you add a record, Excel doesn't insert a row for you. Instead, it adds it in the first row below the existing list. To do that, however, the first row below the list must be blank. If it's not, you'll have to close the data form and insert a row before you add the new record.

Access   **Menu**   Data ➡ Form

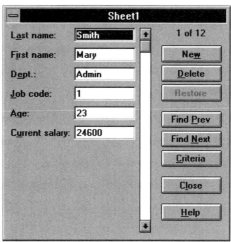

Operation

- To access the data form for a list, the cell pointer must be on a cell in the list.

- To display the next record, click on the Find Next button. To display the previous record, click on the Find Prev button. Use the scroll bar to move to any record in the list.

- To delete the current record, click on the Delete button. Excel will ask you to confirm the operation.

- To modify the current record, type the changes into the text boxes in the data form and press the Enter key. To move from one field to another, press the Tab or Shift+Tab keys. To jump directly to a specific field, hold down the Alt key as you press the underlined character in the field name. To cancel the changes before you press the Enter key, click on the Restore button.

- To add a new record, click on the New button or move the scroll box down beyond the last record in the list. Then, enter the value for each field and press the Enter key. To erase the data from the data form before you press the Enter key, click on the Restore button.

- To select criteria for the records that are displayed, click on the Criteria button. See figure 1-10 for details. Filtering a list before displaying the data form has no effect on the records that are displayed.

Notes

- If a field is protected or is a computed value, it can't be modified and isn't displayed in a text box.

- A data form can display a maximum of 32 fields.

Figure 1-9   **How to use a data form to browse, delete, change, and add records to a list**

How to select the records displayed in the data form

Figure 1-10 shows how you can select the records that are displayed in the data form. Once you specify the criteria for the records you want to display, you can browse through the records using the Find Next and Find Previous buttons. You can also delete or modify selected records using the techniques that were presented in figure 1-9.

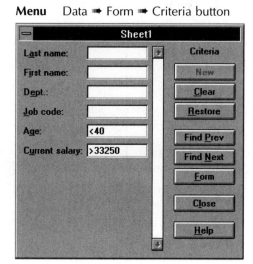

Access   Menu   Data ➡ Form ➡ Criteria button

Operation

- To display selected records, type criteria into the appropriate text boxes. Then, press the Enter key and the first record that satisfies the criteria is displayed. To return to the record display without finding the first record that satisfies the criteria, click on the Form button.

- To display the next record that satisfies the criteria, click on the Find Next button. To display the previous record, click on the Find Prev button.

- To remove the criteria, click on the Clear button. Then, return to the record display by clicking on the Form button.

Note

- You can't use the scroll bar to scroll through the records when you use criteria. If you do, Excel displays all the records in the list, not just those that satisfy the criteria.

Figure 1-10   How to select the records that are displayed in the data form

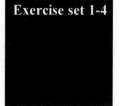

1. Use the techniques for working with data forms presented in figure 1-9 to display the third record in the Employee list and change the Current salary field to 42,000. Next, find the record for Alice Williams and delete it. Finally, add a new record with data of your choice.

2. Use the data form as described in figure 1-10 so that it displays only the records for employees whose current salary is 40,000 or more. Then, close the Employee file without saving the changes.

Perspective

Compared to earlier releases of Excel and to other spreadsheet programs, the list features of Excel 5 are versatile and easy to use. With just the features presented in this chapter, you can quickly create a list and select records from it. For simple list applications, that's all you need to know.

As you'll see in the next three chapters, though, Excel also provides other useful features for working with lists. In chapter 2, you'll learn how to sort the data in a list and add subtotals. And in chapter 3, you'll learn how to summarize the data in a list by creating a pivot table from it.

Finally, in chapter 4, you'll learn how to import data from an external database into an Excel list. Then, you can use the list features of Excel to work with data that's created and maintained by a separate database program. For many spreadsheet users in business, this is the most valuable use of the Excel list features.

Summary

- A *list* is a range of rows in a worksheet that contain similar data. The first row in a list, called the *header row*, contains *column labels* or *field names* that identify the data in each column. The remaining rows represent *records*.

- You can use basic Excel techniques (like inserting and deleting rows and editing the contents of cells) to work with the data in a list.

- The AutoFilter feature lets you display the records in a list that satisfy criteria you select for one or more columns in the list. Records that don't satisfy the criteria are hidden from view, or *filtered*. When you select records based on two or more columns, all of the criteria must be met for a record to be displayed.

- To use a relational operator other than "equals" or to combine two conditions for the same field, you can use the Custom option that's available from the AutoFilter drop-down lists.

- To do a complex selection that AutoFilter can't handle, use the Advanced Filter feature. To use this feature, you have to set up a *criteria range* that defines the records you want to select. Then, you can filter the list so that it displays only those records, or you can create a *results table* that contains only those records.

- The Form command displays a *data form* dialog box that you can use to browse through the records in a list. You can also use a data form to add, delete, and modify records. And by specifying criteria, you can select the records that are displayed in the data form.

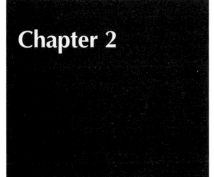

Chapter 2

How to sort and summarize the data in a list

How to sort the data in a list
How to use the Sort command
How to change the normal sort order
How to use the toolbar buttons for sorting
How to retain the original unsorted sequence

How to add automatic subtotals to a list

Perspective

Summary

Introduction

After you set up a list in a worksheet, sorting the data can often make it easier to interpret. The employee list in the top of figure 2-1, for example, is sorted by job code, which makes it easier to compare the employees within each job code. Once you sort the data in a list, you can also summarize the data in the other columns. The list in the bottom of figure 2-1, for example, summarizes the salaries in each job code.

If you already know how to sort the data in a range of cells, you'll have no problem sorting the data in a list. In fact, Excel makes it especially easy to sort the data in a list as you'll see in this chapter. Excel also makes it easy to summarize the data in a list by adding automatic subtotals.

The Employee list created in chapter 1 after it's sorted by job code

	A	B	C	D	E	F	G
1	Last name	First name	Dept.	Job code	Age	Current salary	
2	Smith	Mary	Admin	1	23	$24,600	
3	Williams	Alice	Admin	1	50	$28,900	
4	Thompson	John	Mktg	1	50	$26,500	
5	Burkes	Patricia	Prod	1	52	$28,500	
6	Johnson	Edward	Admin	2	30	$33,250	
7	Allen	Joel	Admin	2	25	$30,000	
8	Clay	Kurt	Mktg	2	43	$41,250	
9	Jones	John	Prod	2	33	$31,400	
10	Russell	Barry	Prod	2	33	$31,500	
11	Andrews	Anne	Admin	3	30	$34,000	
12	Jones	Georgia	Mktg	3	43	$47,500	
13	Long	John	Prod	3	52	$39,900	
14							

The Employee list above after subtotals are added to show the sum of the salaries in each job code

	A	B	C	D	E	F	G
1	Last name	First name	Dept.	Job code	Age	Current salary	
2	Smith	Mary	Admin	1	23	$24,600	
3	Williams	Alice	Admin	1	50	$28,900	
4	Thompson	John	Mktg	1	50	$26,500	
5	Burkes	Patricia	Prod	1	52	$28,500	
6				1 Total		$108,500	
7	Johnson	Edward	Admin	2	30	$33,250	
8	Allen	Joel	Admin	2	25	$30,000	
9	Clay	Kurt	Mktg	2	43	$41,250	
10	Jones	John	Prod	2	33	$31,400	
11	Russell	Barry	Prod	2	33	$31,500	
12				2 Total		$167,400	
13	Andrews	Anne	Admin	3	30	$34,000	
14	Jones	Georgia	Mktg	3	43	$47,500	
15	Long	John	Prod	3	52	$39,900	
16				3 Total		$121,400	
17				Grand Total		$397,300	
18							

Figure 2-1   Examples of a sorted list and a list that contains subtotals

How to sort the data in a list

You can sort the data in a list using either the Sort command in the Data menu or the toolbar buttons for sorting. You'll learn how to use both techniques in the topics that follow.

How to use the Sort command

Figure 2-2 presents the procedure for sorting the data in a list using the Sort command. If the cell pointer is positioned on any cell in the list when you issue this command, Excel automatically recognizes the records in the list as the *data range*. In addition, it uses the column labels in that row to help you identify the sort keys for the list.

For any sort, you have to identify the column you want to use as the *primary sort key*, that is, the column you want to sort the list by. If you want to sort by more than one column, you can identify one or two *secondary sort keys*. The list in figure 2-2, for example, is sorted by department in ascending sequence, and the records in each department are sorted by current salary in descending sequence.

Access   **Menu**   Data ➡ Sort

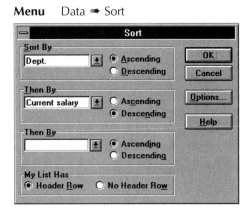

Procedure

1. Place the cell pointer on any cell in the list and access the Sort dialog box.

2. Select the column you want to use as the primary key from the drop-down list box in the Sort By group, and select the Ascending or Descending option from that group.

3. If you want to sort by more than one key, select the column you want to use for each secondary key from the drop-down list box in one of the Then By groups, and select the Ascending or Descending option from that group.

4. Click on the OK button and Excel sorts the list:

	A	B	C	D	E	F	G
1	Last name	First name	Dept.	Job code	Age	Current salary	
2	Andrews	Anne	Admin	3	30	$34,000	
3	Johnson	Edward	Admin	2	30	$33,250	
4	Allen	Joel	Admin	2	25	$30,000	
5	Williams	Alice	Admin	1	50	$28,900	
6	Smith	Mary	Admin	1	23	$24,600	
7	Jones	Georgia	Mktg	3	43	$47,500	
8	Clay	Kurt	Mktg	2	43	$41,250	
9	Thompson	John	Mktg	1	50	$26,500	
10	Long	John	Prod	3	52	$39,900	
11	Russell	Barry	Prod	2	33	$31,500	
12	Jones	John	Prod	2	33	$31,400	
13	Burkes	Patricia	Prod	1	52	$28,500	
14							

Notes

- When Excel recognizes the data as a list, it automatically: (1) sets the My List Has option to Header Row, (2) excludes the header row from the data to be sorted, and (3) uses column labels from the header row in the Sort By and Then By drop-down list boxes.

- The Options button displays another dialog box that lets you specify additional options for the sort operation. See figure 2-4 for details.

- In the unlikely case that you want to sort by more than three key columns, do the sort in two steps. First, sort the list by the least significant keys, then sort again by the more significant keys.

Figure 2-2   How to use the Sort command to sort the data in a list

How to change the normal sort order

When you sort a list based on a column that contains just labels or just values, the sort works the way you would expect. When you sort a list based on a key that contains a mix of labels and values, however, the result isn't as obvious. Figure 2-3 presents the *normal sort order* Excel uses when it sorts a list in ascending sequence. When you sort in descending sequence, the entire sort order is reversed, except empty cells still come last.

Most of the time, Excel's normal sort order will sort the data the way you want it. The only problem might be if you use both uppercase and lowercase letters in a sort column. By default, Excel doesn't distinguish between uppercase and lowercase letters when it does a sort. If you want to override this default, access the Sort Options dialog box as described in figure 2-4 and select the Case Sensitive option. Then, uppercase letters will come before lowercase letters in the sort order. Note that this option affects the sorts you do using the toolbar buttons as well those you do using the Sort command.

The Sort Options dialog box also lets you choose a different sort order altogether or a different sort orientation. Figure 2-4 describes these options. However, it's not likely that you'll ever need to use them.

---

1. Numeric values in sequence (including dates, times, and results of formulas)

2. Labels in this order:

    Digits in numeric sequence
    Space
    Special characters
    Letters in alphabetic sequence

3. Empty cells

Notes

- For a descending sort, this order is reversed, except empty cells are always sorted last.

- By default, sort operations don't distinguish between uppercase and lowercase letters. To override this default, select the Case Sensitive option in the Sort Options dialog box (see figure 2-4).

Figure 2-3   The normal sort order

Access   **Menu**   Data ➡ Sort ➡ Options button

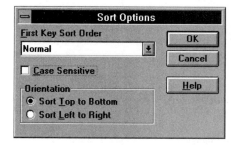

Operation

- To specify that the sort order should distinguish between uppercase and lowercase letters, select the Case Sensitive option. Then, uppercase letters come before lowercase letters in the sort order. For example, AAA comes before aAa, which comes before aaa.

- To use a different sort order for the primary key, choose one of the options in the First Key Sort Order drop-down list box.

- To sort rows based on the contents of a key column, leave the Orientation option set to Sort Top To Bottom. In the unlikely case that you want to sort columns based on the contents of a key row, change the Orientation option setting to Sort Left To Right.

Figure 2-4   How to change the sort order

How to use the toolbar buttons for sorting

Figure 2-5 presents the two buttons in the Standard toolbar that you can use to sort the data in a list. The first button lets you sort in ascending sequence, and the second button lets you sort in descending sequence. When you use either of these buttons to sort a list, you position the cell pointer in the column you want to use as the sort key before you click on the button.

If you use the toolbar buttons to sort a list, you can sort by only one key at a time. If you want to sort a list by more than one key, you can use the Sort command, or you can do each sort in a separate step. Just be sure to sort by the least significant key first and by the most significant key last. If you're sorting by a primary key and one secondary key, for example, sort by the secondary key first. Otherwise, the sort won't work the way you want it to.

How to retain the original unsorted sequence

When you sort the data in a range, it's usually difficult to return the data to its original sequence. That's why you might want to keep two versions of the data: one in its original sequence and one in sorted sequence. To do that, just copy the data to another worksheet before you sort it. Or, if you want to save the two versions in separate files, save the original version, then sort the data and save it with a new file name.

If you don't want to keep two versions of the data, you can add a column of sequence numbers to the list. The easiest way to do that is to use the AutoFill feature. Then, after you sort the data, you can return the list to its original sequence by sorting it again using the column that contains the sequence numbers as the sort key.

Button	Name	Function
A/Z↓	Sort Ascending	Sorts the data in ascending sequence.
Z/A↓	Sort Descending	Sorts the data in descending sequence.

Procedure

1. Place the cell pointer on a cell in the column you want to use as the primary key column. It can be in any row in the list.
2. Click on the appropriate toolbar button.

Notes

- Excel will interpret a range as a list if it has a header row and if at least one blank row and one blank column separate it from other data in the worksheet. If Excel can't interpret the range you want to sort as a list, select the range before you click on the toolbar button. Excel will use the leftmost column in the selection as the primary key.

- You can't sort data by more than one key at a time when you use the toolbar buttons. If you need to sort by more than one key, use the Sort command in the Data menu. Or, do the sort operation in multiple steps, sorting by the least significant key first and the most significant key last.

Figure 2-5   How to use the buttons for sorting in the Standard toolbar

 **Exercise set 2-1**

1. Open the Employee file you created in chapter 1. Then, use the procedure in figure 2-2 to sort the Employee list by job code in ascending order, then by salary in descending order.

2. To illustrate what happens when the Case Sensitive option is selected, change the Dept. field in the record for Joel Allen so that it's in uppercase letters (ADMIN). Then, use the technique in figure 2-4 to select the Case Sensitive option. Finally, use the procedure in figure 2-5 to sort the list by department in ascending order. Notice that the record you changed to contain uppercase letters comes first in the sorted list. Change the Dept. field in this record back to its original value (Admin).

How to add automatic subtotals to a list

Figure 2-6 presents the procedure for adding automatic subtotals to a list. Notice that before you add subtotals, you must sort the list by the column you want Excel to use to determine where the subtotals are inserted. Then, when you issue the Subtotals command, Excel inserts a subtotal line each time the content of that column changes.

In the Subtotal dialog box, you select the column you used to sort the list, the type of summary you want to perform, and the fields you want to summarize. The same type of summary is performed for each field you select. In most cases, you'll use the Count, Sum, or Average function, but you can also select from some basic statistical functions.

Additional information

✓ By default, Excel replaces any subtotals currently in the list with the subtotals you specify. If you want to add subtotals to those that already exist, deselect the Replace Current Subtotals option in the Subtotal dialog box.

✓ If you want subtotals to appear above rather than below groups of rows, deselect the Summary Below Data option in the Subtotal dialog box.

✓ To remove subtotal rows from a list, click on any cell in the list, issue the Subtotals command from the Data menu, and click on the Remove All button.

Access   **Menu**   Data ➡ Subtotals

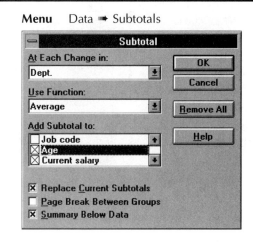

Procedure

1. Sort the list by the column you want Excel to use to determine where to insert subtotal rows.

2. Place the cell pointer on any cell in the list and access the Subtotal dialog box.

3. Select the column you want Excel to use to determine where to insert subtotal rows from the At Each Change In list.

4. Select the function you want Excel to use in the subtotal rows from the Use Function list.

5. Select the fields you want to summarize from the Add Subtotal To list.

6. Click on the OK button, and Excel adds subtotal rows and a grand total row to the list and displays the worksheet in outline form:

		A	B	C	D	E	F	G
	1	Last name	First name	Dept.	Job code	Age	Current salary	
	2	Smith	Mary	Admin	1	23	$24,600	
	3	Johnson	Edward	Admin	2	30	$33,250	
	4	Williams	Alice	Admin	1	50	$28,900	
	5	Allen	Joel	Admin	2	25	$30,000	
	6	Andrews	Anne	Admin	3	30	$34,000	
	7			Admin Average		31.6	$30,150	
	8	Jones	Georgia	Mktg	3	43	$47,500	
	9	Clay	Kurt	Mktg	2	43	$41,250	
	10	Thompson	John	Mktg	1	50	$26,500	
	11			Mktg Average		45.33	$38,417	
	12	Long	John	Prod	3	52	$39,900	
	13	Jones	John	Prod	2	33	$31,400	
	14	Burkes	Patricia	Prod	1	52	$28,500	
	15	Russell	Barry	Prod	2	33	$31,500	
	16			Prod Average		42.5	$32,825	
	17			Grand Average		38.67	$33,108	
	18							

Figure 2-6   How to add automatic subtotals to a sorted list

When you issue the Subtotals command, Excel adds subtotal lines and a grand total line to your list and displays it in outline form. Then, you can use the outline skills presented in figure 2-7 to hide or display information in the list. To remove the subtotal lines and restore the list to its original form, access the Subtotal dialog box and click on the Remove All button.

The list in figure 2-6 after the detail lines for the Mktg and Prod departments were hidden

		A	B	C	D	E	F	G
	1	**Last name**	**First name**	**Dept.**	**Job code**	**Age**	**Current salary**	
	2	Smith	Mary	Admin	1	23	$24,600	
	3	Johnson	Edward	Admin	2	30	$33,250	
	4	Williams	Alice	Admin	1	50	$28,900	
	5	Allen	Joel	Admin	2	25	$30,000	
	6	Andrews	Anne	Admin	3	30	$34,000	
	7			**Admin Average**			$30,150	
	11			**Mktg Average**			$38,417	
	16			**Prod Average**			$32,825	
	17			**Grand Average**			$33,108	
	18							

How to remove an outline

Select the Clear Outline command from the Group and Outline submenu of the Data menu.

Three ways to hide information in an outline

- Click on an outline symbol that shows a number to hide all of the detail information in the outline below that level.

- Click on an outline symbol that shows a minus sign to hide all of the detail information subordinate to the associated outline item.

- Select a cell in a summary row or column for the outline level you want to hide, then select the Hide Detail command from the Group and Outline submenu of the Data menu.

Three ways to show information in an outline

- Click on an outline symbol that shows a number to show all of the information in the outline at that level and above.

- Click on an outline symbol that shows a plus sign to display all of the information at the level directly subordinate to the associated outline item.

- Select a cell in a summary row or column for the outline level you want to expand, then select the Show Detail command from the Group and Outline submenu of the Data menu.

Figure 2-7   How to remove an outline or hide and show information in an outline

Exercise set 2-2

1. Use the procedure in figure 2-6 to add subtotals to the Employee list. The subtotals should show the sum of the salaries for each job code.

2. Click on the button near the upper left corner of the document window with the number 2 in it to hide all the detail records in the list. Next, click on the button with the number 1 in it to hide the subtotals. Then, click on the button to the left of the grand total line with a plus sign in it to redisplay the subtotals. Finally, click on each of the buttons to the left of the subtotal lines to redisplay the detail lines. When you're done, close the Employee file without saving the changes.

Perspective

With Excel, you can easily sort the data in a list. Then, you can add subtotals to the list to summarize the data based on the sort field. The subtotals feature is particularly useful because it lets you choose the fields you want to summarize as well as the function that's used to summarize those fields. Without this feature, you'd have to add a formula to the worksheet for each field in each group of records you wanted to summarize.

Summary

• You can sort the data in a list on one or more *sort keys* using the Sort command in the Data menu. The first sort key you specify is the *primary sort key*. Any additional sort keys you specify are *secondary sort keys*.

• Excel uses a prescribed sequence called the *normal sort order* when it sorts columns whose cells contain a mix of letters, numbers, and special characters.

• You can use toolbar buttons to sort a list, but when you do, you can sort by only one key at a time.

• If you need to work with the data in a list in its original sequence after you sort it, you can save a separate version of the file in unsorted sequence. Or, you can add a column of sequence numbers to the list before you sort it and use them to return the list to its original sequence.

• You can add automatic subtotals to a list by using the Subtotals command in the Data menu.

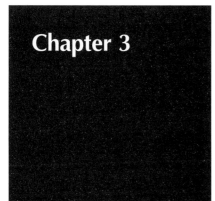

Chapter 3

How to use pivot tables

Basic skills for creating and using pivot tables
    How to create a simple pivot table
    How to change the layout of a pivot table
    How to change the summary function and the format of the summary
        data
    How to change the subtotals in a pivot table
    How to update the contents of a pivot table

Other skills for working with pivot tables
    How to create a more complicated pivot table
    How to hide and show detail data
    How to group numeric items into ranges
    How to use a page field to filter the data in a pivot table

Perspective

Summary

Introduction

A *pivot table* is a table that summarizes the data in one or more fields of a list, an external database, or another pivot table. The two pivot tables in figure 3-1, for example, were created from the Employee list shown at the top of the figure. The first pivot table shows the average salary for three job codes in three departments. You can create a simple pivot table like this in a matter of seconds. The second pivot table in the figure is more complicated. It shows the number of employees in each of the three departments who fall into specific salary ranges. In addition, this pivot table is filtered by job code so that only the employees with job code 2 are included.

Pivot tables are a major new feature of Excel 5. Once you get comfortable with them, you'll be able to use them to create complicated summary reports. So you can get started using pivot tables right away, the first part of this chapter teaches you basic skills for creating and using pivot tables. Then, the second part of this chapter presents some additional skills that will help you create more complicated pivot tables.

The Employee list

	A	B	C	D	E	F	G
1	Last name	First name	Dept.	Job code	Age	Current salary	
2	Smith	Mary	Admin	1	23	$24,600	
3	Jones	Georgia	Mktg	3	43	$47,500	
4	Long	John	Prod	3	52	$39,900	
5	Johnson	Edward	Admin	2	30	$33,250	
6	Jones	John	Prod	2	33	$31,400	
7	Williams	Alice	Admin	1	50	$28,900	
8	Allen	Joel	Admin	2	25	$30,000	
9	Clay	Kurt	Mktg	2	43	$41,250	
10	Burkes	Patricia	Prod	1	52	$28,500	
11	Andrews	Anne	Admin	3	30	$34,000	
12	Russell	Barry	Prod	2	33	$31,500	
13	Thompson	John	Mktg	1	50	$26,500	
14							

A pivot table that shows the average salary for each job code in each department

	A	B	C	D	E	F
1	Average salary	Dept.				
2	Job code	Admin	Mktg	Prod	Grand Total	
3	1	$26,750	$26,500	$28,500	$27,125	
4	2	$31,625	$41,250	$31,450	$33,480	
5	3	$34,000	$47,500	$39,900	$40,467	
6	Grand Total	$30,150	$38,417	$32,825	$33,108	
7						

A pivot table that shows the number of employees in each department with job code 2 that fall within the given salary ranges

	A	B	C	D	E	F
1	Job code	2 ⬇				
2						
3	Number of employees	Dept.				
4	Current salary	Mktg	Admin	Prod	Grand Total	
5	30000-31000	0	1	0	1	
6	31000-32000	0	0	2	2	
7	33000-34000	0	1	0	1	
8	41000-42000	1	0	0	1	
9	Grand Total	1	2	2	5	
10						

Figure 3-1   Two pivot tables created from the Employee list

Basic skills for creating and using pivot tables

To help you understand the concepts and skills required to create and use pivot tables, you'll begin by learning how to create a simple pivot table like the one in figure 3-1. Then, you'll learn how to change the layout of a pivot table, how to change the summary function and the format of the summary data, how to change the subtotal function, and how to update the contents of a pivot table. Once you're comfortable with these procedures, you'll be ready to learn how to create more complicated pivot tables and use the other skills presented in this chapter.

Although you can create and work with pivot tables using commands in the Data and short-cut menus and their submenus, Excel also provides a toolbar specifically for working with pivot tables. Figure 3-2 presents the Query and Pivot toolbar and describes its buttons. If Excel doesn't display this toolbar automatically, you can use the Toolbars command in the View menu to display it.

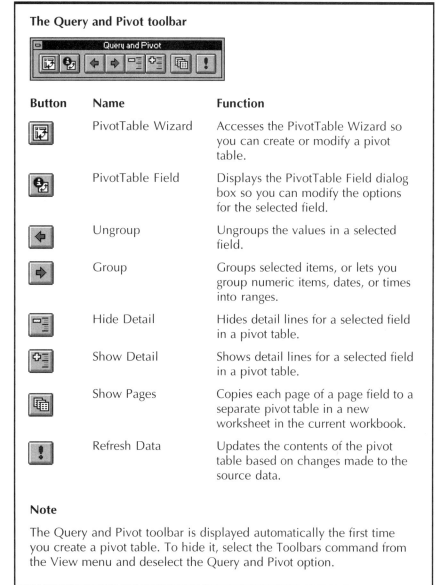

The Query and Pivot toolbar

Button	Name	Function
	PivotTable Wizard	Accesses the PivotTable Wizard so you can create or modify a pivot table.
	PivotTable Field	Displays the PivotTable Field dialog box so you can modify the options for the selected field.
	Ungroup	Ungroups the values in a selected field.
	Group	Groups selected items, or lets you group numeric items, dates, or times into ranges.
	Hide Detail	Hides detail lines for a selected field in a pivot table.
	Show Detail	Shows detail lines for a selected field in a pivot table.
	Show Pages	Copies each page of a page field to a separate pivot table in a new worksheet in the current workbook.
	Refresh Data	Updates the contents of the pivot table based on changes made to the source data.

Note

The Query and Pivot toolbar is displayed automatically the first time you create a pivot table. To hide it, select the Toolbars command from the View menu and deselect the Query and Pivot option.

Figure 3-2   The Query and Pivot toolbar

How to create a simple pivot table

When you create a pivot table, you use Excel's PivotTable Wizard. Because the PivotTable Wizard walks you through the steps, creating a pivot table is as easy as selecting the fields you want it to contain. Figure 3-3 presents the procedure for using this feature.

The first dialog box asks you to identify the type of source data you want to summarize. Although Excel lets you create a pivot table from four different sources, you'll usually use the default: an Excel list. Then, the next dialog box prompts you for the range that contains the list. If you place the cell pointer on a cell in the list before you start the PivotTable Wizard, Excel will enter the correct range for you. Otherwise, you can type in the range or select it in the worksheet.

If you choose to create a pivot table from a source other than a list, the second PivotTable Wizard dialog box changes accordingly. If you select the External Data Source option, for example, the dialog box asks you if you want to start Microsoft Query to retrieve the data from an external data source. You'll learn how to use Microsoft Query in chapter 4.

Once you identify the data, you're ready to set up the pivot table. To do that, drag the buttons that represent the fields in the list into the appropriate areas of the pivot table diagram in the third dialog box. If you drag a field into the Column area, it becomes a *column field*. If you drag a field into the Row area, it becomes a *row field*. The column and row fields identify the fields by which the data is summarized. In figure

Procedure

1. Place the cell pointer on a cell in the list you want to create the pivot table from.

2. Select the PivotTable command from the Data menu, or click on the PivotTable Wizard toolbar button. Then, this dialog box appears:

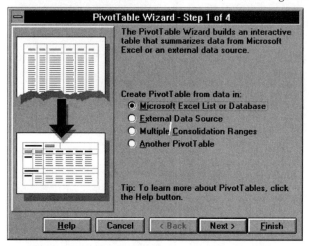

3. Click on the Next button to create the pivot table from a list, and this dialog box appears:

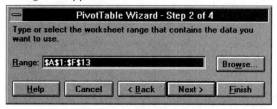

4. Make sure that the range that's displayed for the list is correct, then click on the Next button and this dialog box appears:

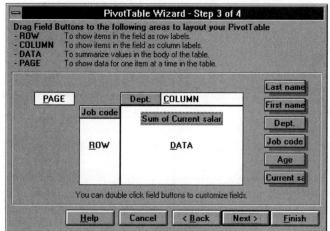

Drag the buttons for the fields you want to include in the pivot table to the proper locations as described at the top of the dialog box.

Figure 3-3   How to create a pivot table from a list (part 1 of 2)

3-3, the data is summarized by job code and department. If you drag a field into the Data area, it becomes a *data field*. The data field identifies the field to be summarized, in this case, the current salary.

The last PivotTable Wizard dialog box lets you specify four pivot table options. All four of these options are selected by default, which is usually what you want. You can also indicate where you want Excel to place the pivot table by specifying a cell reference in the PivotTable Starting Cell text box. The default is to place the pivot table in a new worksheet in the current workbook. Finally, you can change the name Excel assigns to the pivot table from this dialog box.

If you study the pivot table created in figure 3-3, you'll see that the subcategories for each row and column field you selected are included as column or row labels in the pivot table. These labels are called *pivot table items*; they indicate the categories of data that are summarized in the table. For example, the Dept. column field contains three pivot table items: Admin, Mktg, and Prod.

The *summary function* that's used in a pivot table depends on the data field you're summarizing. If the data field is numeric, the default is to use the Sum function. If the data field contains text, the default is to use the Count function. The data field I selected in figure 3-3 contains employee salaries, so the pivot table shows the sum of the current salaries for each job code in each department.

5. Click on the Next button and this dialog box appears:

6. Deselect any options in the PivotTable Options group that aren't appropriate. Then, click on the Finish button and Excel builds the pivot table according to your specifications:

	A	B	C	D	E	F
1	Sum of Current salary	Dept.				
2	Job code	Admin	Mktg	Prod	Grand Total	
3	1	53500	26500	28500	108500	
4	2	63250	41250	62900	167400	
5	3	34000	47500	39900	121400	
6	Grand Total	150750	115250	131300	397300	
7						

Notes

- The default summary function for a numeric field is Sum. The default summary function for a non-numeric field is Count. See figure 3-5 for details on how to change these functions.

- Excel automatically adds subtotals and grand totals to a pivot table when you create it, so you should remove any subtotals from a list before you create a pivot table from it. If you don't want to include grand totals, deselect the Grand Totals For Rows and Grand Totals For Columns options.

- By default, Excel places the pivot table in a new worksheet at the end of the current workbook. (If you use Excel's default of 16 worksheets in a workbook, that means the pivot table is placed in worksheet 17.) If you want to, you can supply a specific location in the PivotTable Starting Cell text box in the last dialog box.

- When you create a pivot table, no direct link is maintained between the pivot table and the data it is based on. Instead, Excel creates a copy of the source data and uses that copy whenever you make changes to the pivot table. The Save Data With Table Layout option in the last dialog box determines whether or not that copy is saved with the pivot table when you close the workbook. The default is to save the data, but if the data is extensive, that may not be what you want. If you don't save the data, however, you have to refresh the pivot table as described later in this chapter before you can make any changes to it.

- If you don't want to use Excel's default autoformat for the pivot table, deselect the AutoFormat Table option in the last dialog box.

Figure 3-3   **How to create a pivot table from a list (part 2 of 2)**

How to change the layout of a pivot table

The row and column fields you select for a pivot table and the sequence of the pivot table items within those fields determine the layout of the pivot table. If the pivot table doesn't look the way you want it to when you create it, you can change the layout. In fact, the name pivot table is based on the fact that you can "pivot" row and column fields around the data area to look at the summary data in different ways.

Figure 3-4 shows you how to change the layout of a pivot table by moving column and row fields and pivot table items. The easiest way to move a field or item is to drag it to a new location in the table. To create the pivot table in figure 3-4, for example, I dragged the Dept. label so that it's now a row field instead of a column field, and I dragged the Admin item so it's now after the Mktg item. You can also move a row or column field from the third PivotTable Wizard dialog box. Just drag the button for the field to a new location in the pivot table area.

How to move a column or row field with the mouse

Drag the label for a column or row field to a new position. As you drag the label, the pointer indicates whether the field will be a column or a row field, and the insert marker indicates where the field will be inserted:

	A	B	C	D	E	F
1	Sum of Current salary	Dept.				
2	Job code	Admin	Mktg	Prod	Grand Total	
3	1	53500	26500	28500	108500	
4	2	63250	41250	62900	167400	
5	3	34000	47500	39900	121400	
6	Grand Total	150750	115250	131300	397300	
7						

How to move a column or row field with the PivotTable command

1. With the cell pointer on any cell in the pivot table, access the PivotTable Wizard and the third PivotTable Wizard dialog box appears.

2. Drag the button for a column or row field to a new position.

3. Click on the Finish button, and Excel changes the layout of the pivot table based on the new position of the field.

How to move a pivot table item

1. Place the cell pointer on the cell that contains the label for the item you want to move.

2. Place the mouse pointer on the border of the cell so it turns into an arrow.

3. Drag the item to a new location:

	A	B	C	D	E	F
1	Sum of Current salary	Dept.				
2	Job code	Admin	Mktg	Prod	Grand Total	
3	1	53500	26500	28500	108500	
4	2	63250	41250	62900	167400	
5	3	34000	47500	39900	121400	
6	Grand Total	150750	115250	131300	397300	
7						

The pivot table in figure 3-3 after the Dept. column field was changed to a row field and the Dept. items were resequenced

	A	B	C	D
1	Sum of Current salary			
2	Dept.	Job code	Total	
3	Mktg	1	26500	
4		2	41250	
5		3	47500	
6	Mktg Total		115250	
7	Admin	1	53500	
8		2	63250	
9		3	34000	
10	Admin Total		150750	
11	Prod	1	28500	
12		2	62900	
13		3	39900	
14	Prod Total		131300	
15	Grand Total		397300	
16				

Figure 3-4   How to change the layout of a pivot table

How to change the summary function and the format of the summary data

Figure 3-5 shows you how to use the PivotTable Field dialog box for a data field to customize a pivot table. From this dialog box, you can select from a variety of functions for summarizing the data in the pivot table. You can also change the format of the data by clicking on the Number button and selecting a format from the Format Cells dialog box that appears. And you can change the name that's used in the pivot table to describe the summary. The pivot table at the bottom of the figure shows the pivot table created in figure 3-4 after the summary function was changed to Average and a Currency format was selected.

Access	Menu	Data ➡ PivotTable Field
	Shortcut menu	PivotTable Field
	Query and Pivot toolbar	

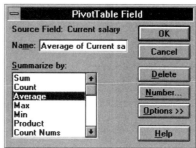

Operation

- To access the PivotTable Field dialog box shown above, the cell pointer must be on a cell in the data area or on the cell that contains the label that describes the summary.

- To change the summary function, select a function from the Summarize By list box.

- To change the name of the summary field, enter a new value in the Name text box. You can also change the name of a summary field by selecting the cell that contains the name and entering a new value.

- To specify the number format for the summary data, click on the Number button and complete the Format Cells dialog box that appears.

The pivot table in figure 3-4 after the summary function was changed to Average and a Currency format was applied

	A	B	C	D
1	Average of Current salary			
2	Dept.	Job code	Total	
3	Mktg	1	$26,500	
4		2	$41,250	
5		3	$47,500	
6	Mktg Total		$38,417	
7	Admin	1	$26,750	
8		2	$31,625	
9		3	$34,000	
10	Admin Total		$30,150	
11	Prod	1	$28,500	
12		2	$31,450	
13		3	$39,900	
14	Prod Total		$32,825	
15	Grand Total		$33,108	
16				

Notes

- You can also access the PivotTable Field dialog box from the PivotTable Wizard. To do that, double-click on the button for the data field in the data area of the third PivotTable Wizard dialog box.

- If you click on the Options button, Excel displays some additional options that let you specify advanced summarization features.

Figure 3-5   **How to change the summary data**

How to change the subtotals in a pivot table

By default, the subtotals Excel adds to a pivot table use the same function that's used to summarize the data fields. For example, when I changed the summary function in figure 3-5 from Sum to Average, Excel changed the subtotal function as well. To change the subtotal function so that it's different from the summary function, you use the PivotTable Field dialog box shown in figure 3-6. From this dialog box, you can select one or more subtotal functions to be included in the pivot table, or you can remove the subtotals entirely. Note that the functions you select affect only the subtotals and not the grand totals. The grand totals always use the same function as the summary data.

You can also use the PivotTable Field dialog box in figure 3-6 to remove specific items from the pivot table. To do that, just highlight the items in the Hide Items list box. Then, the items are removed from the pivot table and are not included in the subtotals or grand totals.

Additional information

✓ The PivotTable Field dialog box for a column or row field also lets you change the name of the field or delete the field. To change the name, enter the new name in the Name text box. To delete the field, click on the Delete button.

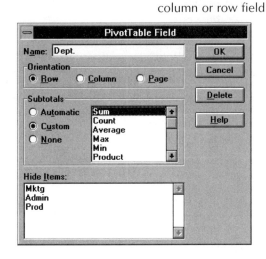

				Menu	Data ➠ PivotTable Field

Access

Menu	Data ➠ PivotTable Field
Shortcut menu	PivotTable Field
Query and Pivot toolbar	
Other	Double-click on the cell that contains the label for the column or row field

Operation

• To access the PivotTable Field dialog box shown above, the cell pointer must be on the cell that contains the label for a column or row field.

• To change the subtotal function, select the Custom option in the Subtotals group, then select a function from the Subtotals list box. If you select more than one function, Excel adds subtotals for each function. To change the subtotal function back to its default, select the Automatic option. To hide subtotals, select the None option.

• To hide one or more items in the field, highlight the items in the Hide Items list box.

The pivot table in figure 3-5 after the subtotals function was changed to Sum

	A	B	C
1	Average of Current salary		
2	Dept.	Job code	Total
3	Mktg	1	$26,500
4		2	$41,250
5		3	$47,500
6	Mktg Sum		$115,250
7	Admin	1	$26,750
8		2	$31,625
9		3	$34,000
10	Admin Sum		$150,750
11	Prod	1	$28,500
12		2	$31,450
13		3	$39,900
14	Prod Sum		$131,300
15	Grand Total		$33,108

Figure 3-6   How to change the subtotals in a pivot table

How to update the contents of a pivot table

If the source data that's summarized in a pivot table changes, the pivot table isn't automatically updated. To update a pivot table so it reflects the current state of the source data, you use the Refresh Data command. This command is available from the Data menu, the shortcut menu, and the Query and Pivot toolbar.

When you refresh a pivot table based on an Excel list, you should know that only the cells in the source range you specified when you created the table are examined. If the source list has more rows or columns than it did when the pivot table was created, you'll need to update the source range for the table before you update its contents. To update the source range, access the PivotTable Wizard to display the layout dialog box, then click on the Back button to display the dialog box that lets you specify the source range.

Exercise set 3-1

1. Open the Employee file you created in chapter 1. Then, use the procedure in figure 3-3 to create a pivot table that summarizes the age of the employees in the Employee list based on department and job code. The departments should be displayed across the top of the pivot table, and the job codes should be displayed down the left side of the table. All of the default options should be used.

2. Use the techniques in figure 3-4 to change the Dept. field from a column field to a row field and to move the Prod department item before the Mktg item.

3. Use the techniques in figure 3-5 to change the summary function for the age field so the average age for each department and job code is displayed and so the average age is displayed as a whole number.

4. Use the technique in figure 3-6 to change the subtotals so that a count of the employees in each department is displayed in addition to the average age.

5. Switch to the worksheet that contains the Employee list and change the age of Mary Smith from 23 to 33. Switch back to the pivot table and use the Refresh Data command to update its contents. Note that the average age of the employees in the Admin department with job code 1 changes from 37 to 42, and the average age of all the employees in the Admin department changes from 32 to 34. Change the age of Mary Smith back to 23 and update the contents of the list again.

Other skills for working with pivot tables

The rest of this chapter presents additional skills you can use to create and work with more sophisticated pivot tables. First, you'll learn how to create pivot tables that contain more than one column, row, and data field. Then, you'll learn three skills that will make it easier for you to work with large or complicated pivot tables: how to hide and show detail data, how to group numeric data into ranges, and how to filter a pivot table using a page field.

How to create a more complicated pivot table

In figure 3-4, you learned how to change the layout of an existing pivot table. However, you're not limited to simply rearranging the fields and items in a pivot table. You can also add column, row, and data fields to create a more complicated pivot table. And you can delete fields you no longer want to include in the table. Of course, you can also create a more complicated pivot table from scratch using the procedure presented in figure 3-3.

Figure 3-7 presents a pivot table that contains one row and one column field and four data fields. You can also create pivot tables that contain two or more row and column fields. However, keep in mind that the more fields you include in a pivot table, the more difficult it will be to interpret. As a result, it makes sense to keep pivot tables relatively simple.

A layout for a pivot table with four data fields

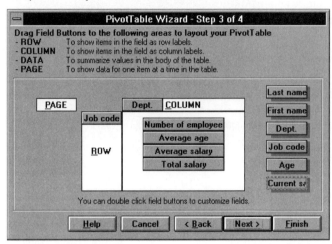

The resulting pivot table

	A	B	C	D	E	F	G
1			Dept.				
2	Job code	Data	Admin	Mktg	Prod	Grand Total	
3	1	Number of employees	2	1	1	4	
4		Average age	37	50	52	44	
5		Average salary	$26,750	$26,500	$28,500	$27,125	
6		Total salary	$53,500	$26,500	$28,500	$108,500	
7	2	Number of employees	2	1	2	5	
8		Average age	28	43	33	33	
9		Average salary	$31,625	$41,250	$31,450	$33,480	
10		Total salary	$63,250	$41,250	$62,900	$167,400	
11	3	Number of employees	1	1	1	3	
12		Average age	30	43	52	42	
13		Average salary	$34,000	$47,500	$39,900	$40,467	
14		Total salary	$34,000	$47,500	$39,900	$121,400	
15	Total Number of employees		5	3	4	12	
16	Total Average age		32	45	43	39	
17	Total Average salary		$30,150	$38,417	$32,825	$33,108	
18	Total Total salary		$150,750	$115,250	$131,300	$397,300	
19							

Operation

- To add a row, column, or data field to a pivot table from the PivotTable Wizard dialog box, drag the button for the field to the proper location in the pivot table area. To delete a row, column, or data field, drag the button for the field out of the pivot table area. You can also delete a row or column field without accessing the PivotTable Wizard by dragging the label for the field outside of the pivot table.

Notes

- You can use a different summary function for each data field in a pivot table. To change a summary function from its default, use the procedure in figure 3-5.

- You can include the same data field in a pivot table more than once. Then, you can specify a different summary function for each occurrence of the field.

Figure 3-7   How to set up a more complicated pivot table

How to hide and show detail data

Figure 3-8 shows you how to hide and show different levels of data in a pivot table. To hide or show the subordinates for a pivot table item, simply double-click on the cell that contains the label for the item. If you prefer, you can also use the Hide Detail and Show Detail commands to hide and show the detail data for a single item or for all the items in a field at once.

You can also display the source data for a value in the data area by double-clicking on the cell that contains the value. Then, Excel displays the records in the list that were used to calculate the value in a separate worksheet. This is an easy way to check the source of the data if you're confused by the results.

How to hide and show details

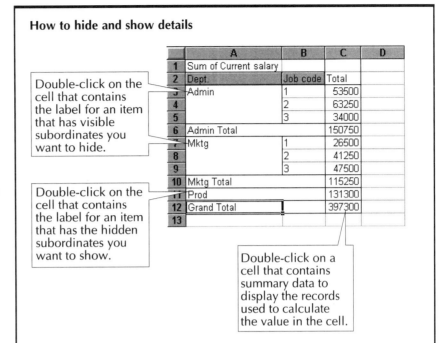

Double-click on the cell that contains the label for an item that has visible subordinates you want to hide.

Double-click on the cell that contains the label for an item that has the hidden subordinates you want to show.

Double-click on a cell that contains summary data to display the records used to calculate the value in the cell.

The records that are displayed when you double-click on the cell in the worksheet above that contains the summary value for job code 2 in the Admin department

	A	B	C	D	E	F	G
1	Last name	First name	Dept.	Job code	Age	Current salary	
2	Johnson	Edward	Admin	2	30	33250	
3	Allen	Joel	Admin	2	25	30000	
4							

Notes

- You can also use the Hide Detail and Show Detail commands in the Group and Outline submenu of the Data or shortcut menu or the Hide Detail and Show Detail buttons in the Query and Pivot toolbar to hide and show detail data. Just move the cell pointer to the cell that contains the label for the item that has subordinate items you want to hide or show, then issue the command.

- To hide or show the details for all the items in a field, move the cell pointer to the cell that contains the label for the field, then issue the Hide Detail or Show Detail command.

- The records used to calculate a value in the data area are displayed in a new worksheet at the end of the workbook.

Figure 3-8   How to hide and show details in a pivot table

How to group numeric items into ranges

Figure 3-9 presents the procedure for grouping numeric items into ranges. In this figure, I grouped the items in the Current salary field into ranges of 10,000 dollars each. As you can see from the resulting pivot table, using ranges can help you interpret the data in a pivot table more easily. This feature is particularly useful when a pivot table field contains many separate values.

Additional information

✓ The first time you display the Grouping dialog box for a field, the Auto check boxes are selected and the values for the Starting At and Ending At options are set to the lowest and highest values in the field. If you change these values, the check boxes are deselected. To return the options to their default values, click on the check boxes.

✓ To redisplay data in ungrouped form, select any cell that contains data for the group. Then, issue the Ungroup command from the Group and Outline submenu of the Data or shortcut menu, or click on the Ungroup button in the Query and Pivot toolbar.

✓ You can also group dates and times into ranges, and you can create groups of selected items. For details, refer to Excel's online Help.

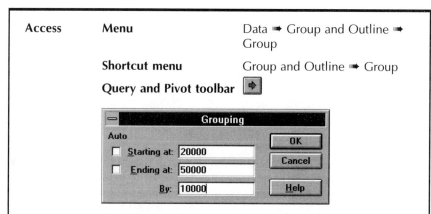

Access	Menu	Data ➡ Group and Outline ➡ Group
	Shortcut menu	Group and Outline ➡ Group
	Query and Pivot toolbar	

Procedure

1. Place the cell pointer on a cell that contains one of the numeric items you want to group:

	A	B	C	D
1	Number of employees			
2	Dept.	Current salary	Total	
3	Admin	24600	1	
4		28900	1	
5		30000	1	
6		33250	1	
7		34000	1	
8	Admin Total		5	
9	Mktg	26500	1	
10		41250	1	
11		47500	1	
12	Mktg Total		3	
13	Prod	28500	1	
14		31400	1	
15		31500	1	
16		39900	1	
17	Prod Total		4	
18	Grand Total		12	
19				

2. Access the Grouping dialog box.

3. Enter values for the Starting At, Ending At, and By options to define the ranges for the field. Then, click on the OK button and the pivot table is changed to reflect the new ranges:

	A	B	C	D
1	Number of employees			
2	Dept.	Current salary	Total	
3	Admin	20000-30000	2	
4		30000-40000	3	
5	Admin Total		5	
6	Mktg	20000-30000	1	
7		40000-50000	2	
8	Mktg Total		3	
9	Prod	20000-30000	1	
10		30000-40000	3	
11	Prod Total		4	
12	Grand Total		12	
13				

Figure 3-9   How to group numeric items into ranges

How to use a page field to filter the data in a pivot table

In chapter 1, you learned how to use the AutoFilter feature to filter the data in a list. Excel provides a similar feature for filtering the data in a pivot table. To implement this feature, you use *page fields*.

Figure 3-10 shows you how to use a page field to filter the data in a pivot table. To create a page field, you access the layout dialog box of the PivotTable Wizard, then drag the field you want to filter into the Page area. When you click on the Finish button, Excel displays the field at the top of the pivot table along with a drop-down list box that contains all the items in that field. The pivot table in step 2 of figure 3-10, for example, contains a page field for the job code. To filter the table, you select an item from the drop-down list for the page field. The pivot table in step 3 of the figure, for example, shows the data for job code 1.

Additional information

✓ You can also create a page field from an existing column or row field by dragging the label for that field above the pivot table to the area where the page fields are displayed. The pointer will indicate when the field is in the correct position.

Procedure

1. Drag the button for the field you want to use as the page field to the Page area of the third PivotTable Wizard dialog box:

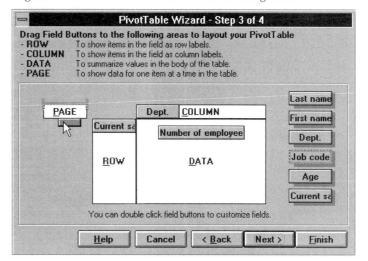

2. Click on the Finish button, and the page field appears with a drop-down list box at the top of the pivot table:

	A	B	C	D	E	F
1	Job code	(All) ⬇				
2						
3	Number of employees	Dept.				
4	Current salary	Admin	Mktg	Prod	Grand Total	
5	24600	1	0	0	1	
6	26500	0	1	0	1	
7	28500	0	0	1	1	
8	28900	1	0	0	1	
9	30000	1	0	0	1	
10	31400	0	0	1	1	
11	31500	0	0	1	1	
12	33250	1	0	0	1	
13	34000	1	0	0	1	
14	39900	0	0	1	1	
15	41250	0	1	0	1	
16	47500	0	1	0	1	
17	Grand Total	5	3	4	12	
18						

3. Select a value from the list to display the data only for that value:

	A	B	C	D	E	F
1	Job code	1 ⬇				
2						
3	Number of employees	Dept.				
4	Current salary	Admin	Mktg	Prod	Grand Total	
5	24600	1	0	0	1	
6	26500	0	1	0	1	
7	28500	0	0	1	1	
8	28900	1	0	0	1	
9	Grand Total	2	1	1	4	
10						

Note

• A pivot table can include more than one page field.

Figure 3-10   How to use a page field to filter a pivot table

Exercise set 3-2

1. Use the techniques in figure 3-7 to add two summary fields to the pivot table you created in exercise set 3-1: the count of employees and the average salary. (You can use either the first name or last name field to count the number of employees.) Then, change the title of the count field to "Number of employees," format the average salary data as currency, and remove the subtotals from the list.

2. Double-click on the cell that contains the label for the Admin department to hide the detail data for that department. Notice that all three of the summary functions are displayed for the department. Now, double-click on the cell that contains the average of the current salaries in the Admin department to display the records for the employees in that department. Return to the worksheet that contains the pivot table by clicking on the appropriate worksheet tab. Double-click on the cell that contains the label for the Admin department to redisplay the data for that department.

3. Use the techniques in figure 3-7 to change the pivot table so that it shows a count of the ages of each employee in each department. (Dept. and Age are the row fields and Count of employees is the summary field.) Use the procedure in figure 3-9 to group the ages from 20 to 60 in increments of 10.

4. Use the procedure in figure 3-10 to change the Dept. field to a page field. Use the page field to filter the pivot table so that only the data in the Admin department is displayed. Close the Employee file, saving the changes if you wish.

Perspective

The pivot table functions presented in this chapter are probably more than you'll need for most of the pivot tables you create. Even so, all of these functions can be useful in particular situations. So if you plan on working with pivot tables, you should spend some time experimenting with this feature. Although some of the functions may seem confusing at first, they'll make more sense once you see how they work.

Summary

- A *pivot table* is a table that summarizes the data in one or more fields of a list, an external database, or another pivot table based on other fields. A pivot table contains *row* and *column fields* that specify the fields by which the data is summarized and *data fields* that determine what data is summarized. You can select from several *summary functions* for each data field.

- You use the PivotTable Wizard to define a pivot table. By default, Excel creates the pivot table in a new worksheet in the current workbook.

- You can change the layout of a pivot table by dragging the labels for row and column fields or pivot table items from one position to another. You can also move row and column fields using the PivotTable Wizard.

- From the PivotTable Field dialog box for a data field, you can select a different summary function for the field, you can specify the format for the summarized data, and you can change the label that's used in the pivot table to identify the summary.

- From the PivotTable Field dialog box for a row or column field, you can change the subtotal function or remove the subtotals.

- To update a pivot table to reflect changes made to the source data it's based on, use the Refresh Data command in the Data or shortcut menu or the Refresh Data button in the Query and Pivot toolbar.

- To hide and show detail data in a pivot table and group numeric items into ranges, use the commands in the Group and Outline submenu of the Data or shortcut menu or the appropriate buttons in the Query and Pivot toolbar.

- You can use a *page field* to filter the data in a pivot table.

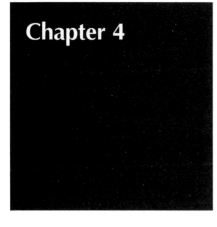

Chapter 4

How to use Microsoft Query to import data from an external database

Because Excel's list feature is flexible and easy to use, more and more people are using it to access and manipulate data from external databases. The most powerful facility Excel 5 provides for accessing this type of data is *Microsoft Query*. Although *Query* is a separate program, it comes with Excel, and the two are tightly integrated.

When you access data from an external database using Query, you can select the fields and records you need and import the data into Excel as a list. That's what you'll learn how to do in this chapter. Then, you can use the list techniques you've already learned to work with the data in Excel.

To access and retrieve data from an external database, Query requires an *ODBC (open database connectivity) driver* for the program that created and manages the database. ODBC drivers for the most popular database programs, such as *dBase*, *FoxPro*, *Access*, *Paradox*, and *SQL Server,* come with Excel, and you can install them during set up. In addition, you can obtain ODBC drivers for other database programs, such as *Btrieve* and *Oracle*, from Microsoft. You can also expect the developers of other database programs to distribute ODBC drivers for their applications.

Basic skills for using Microsoft Query
> How Query works as an interface between Excel and an external database
> How to use Query to access an external database from Excel
> How to perform a simple query
> How to edit a query or update its results
> How to work in the Query window
> How to use the Query menus and toolbar buttons

Other ways to create a query
> How to select fields
> How to select records
> How to edit and delete criteria

Other skills for using Microsoft Query
> How to sort the records in the data pane
> How to create a query using fields from two or more tables
> How to enable the Query add-in program

Perspective

Summary

Basic skills for using Microsoft Query

The first part of this chapter presents the basic skills you need to use Microsoft Query. In addition, it presents the concepts you need to understand how Excel and Query work together to retrieve data from an external database. Once you understand these concepts and skills, you can read the rest of this chapter to learn additional techniques and skills for working with Microsoft Query.

How Query works as an interface between Excel and an external database

Figure 4-1 illustrates how Query works as an interface between Excel and an external database. In general, there are two different types of databases you can access with Query. In a *relational database*, each database file contains one or more related *tables*. When you work with this type of database, it's easy to access data from two or more tables at the same time. In a *non-relational database*, each table is stored in a separate file, called a *flat file*. Most flat files are designed to stand on their own, so you usually won't access more than one flat file at a time.

When you *query* a database, the results of the query are returned to the Query program. Then, you can manipulate and format the data in Query. When you have the data the way you want it, you transfer it to Excel.

Note that the data that's returned to Excel is a copy of the data in the external database. There's no direct link between the data in Excel and the data in the external database. However, if you save the query with the data that's copied to Excel, you can update the data based on changes made to the external database, and you can edit the query to request different data.

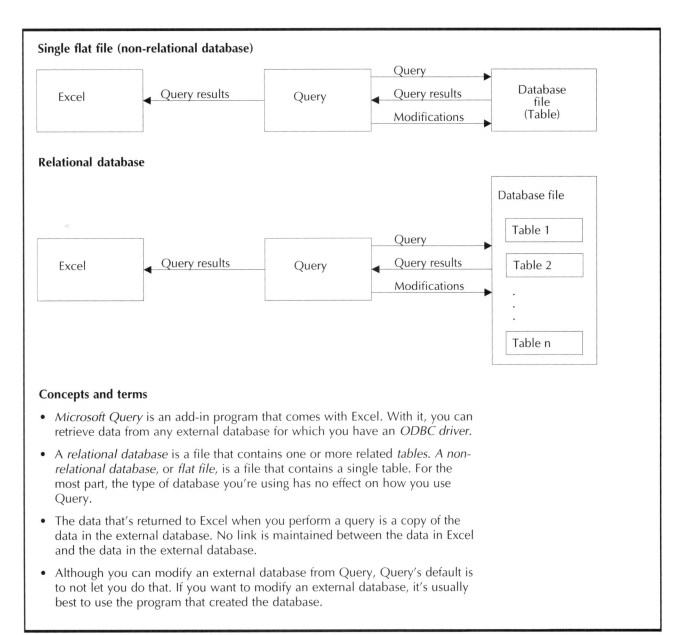

Figure 4-1   How Query works as an interface between Excel and an external database

How to use Query to access an external database from Excel

Figure 4-2 presents two procedures for accessing an external database from Excel. The procedure you use depends on whether you're accessing a relational or a non-relational database. For either type of database, you begin by starting Query and specifying the type of external data you want to access. Then, for a relational database, you identify a specific database file and a table within that file. For a non-relational database, you specify only the file. Then, Query opens the table or file and displays a list of its fields in the *tables pane* at the top of the window. At that point, you're ready to retrieve records from the external database.

Before I go on, you should know that the command you use to start Query, Get External Data, will only appear in the Data menu if the Query add-in program is properly installed and enabled. If this command doesn't appear, you can refer to figure 4-14 to find out how to add it to the menu.

Additional information

✓ If the source of the data you want to use isn't displayed in the Select Data Source dialog box, click on the Other button and select the source from the list that's displayed to add it to the list of data sources.

✓ You can select two or more tables from the Add Tables dialog box. This is useful if you want to retrieve data from two or more tables. See figure 4-12 for more information.

How to access a relational database

1. Place the cell pointer in the worksheet where you want to put the data from the external database. Then, select the Get External Data command from the Data menu to start Query, and this dialog box appears:

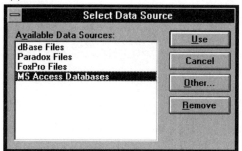

2. Select an option from the Available Data Sources list box to identify the kind of external data you want to retrieve. Click on the Use button, and this dialog box appears:

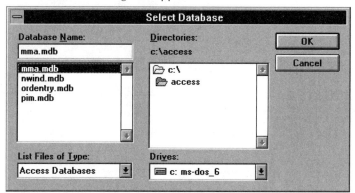

3. Select the database that contains the table you want to access, and this dialog box appears:

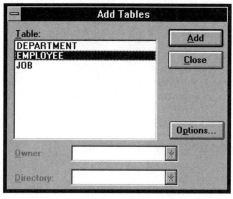

Figure 4-2   **How to use Query to access an external database (part 1 of 2)**

4. Select the table you want to access by double-clicking on it or by highlighting it and clicking on the Add button. Click on the Close button, and Query accesses the table and displays its fields in a field list in the tables pane at the top of the document window:

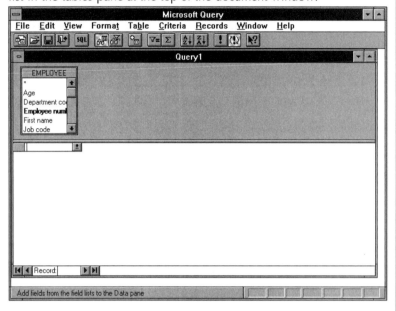

Additional information

✓ If the data source you select is for a relational database and you've already accessed a database of the same type during the current Excel session, Query assumes you want to access the same database and doesn't display the Select Database dialog box. To access a different database, click on the Other button and select the data source to add it to the Select Data Source dialog box a second time. Select the second of the two data sources, and Query displays the Select Database dialog box.

✓ You can also access Query from the PivotTable Wizard. To do that, select the External Data Source option from the first PivotTable Wizard dialog box and click on the Get Data button in the next dialog box that appears. Then, use the techniques presented in this chapter to select the fields and records you want. See chapter 3 for details on how to use the PivotTable Wizard.

✓ Query provides a feature called Cue Cards that steps you through the process of creating a query. The first time you access Query from Excel, a dialog box is displayed that asks you if you want to use Cue Cards. If you don't want this dialog box displayed each time you access Query, select the appropriate option and close the dialog box. If you want to use Cue Cards later, select the Cue Cards command from the Help menu.

How to access a non-relational database

1. Follow the procedure above for selecting a data source. Then, this dialog box appears:

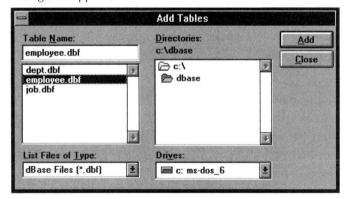

2. Select the file you want to access by double-clicking on it or by highlighting it and clicking on the Add button. Click on the Close button, and Query accesses the file and displays its fields in the field list.

Figure 4-2   How to use Query to access an external database (part 2 of 2)

How to perform a simple query

Once you have access to an external database, you can select the fields and records you want to retrieve and return them to Excel. Figure 4-3 presents the procedure for doing that. Notice that as you select fields, Query displays the data in those fields for each record in the database in the *data pane* at the bottom of the window. As you enter selection criteria, they're displayed in the *criteria pane* in the middle of the window, and any records that don't match the criteria are removed from the data pane.

When you're done selecting the fields and records you want, you return the data to Excel. Then, Excel displays a dialog box that offers several options and lets you specify where you want to place the retrieved data. In most cases, you'll want to accept the defaults for this dialog box. If you do, Excel inserts the data from the external database into the current worksheet, where it's formatted as a list.

Procedure

1. From Query, select the fields you want to retrieve by double-clicking on the field names in the field list or by dragging the field names from the field list into the data pane in the lower part of the window:

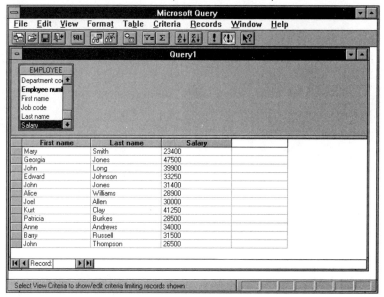

2. To specify selection criteria for the records to be retrieved, select the Add Criteria command from the Criteria menu and this dialog box appears:

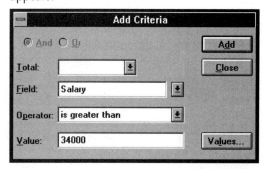

3. For the first criterion, select a field and a relational operator, enter a comparison value, and click on the Add button. For each additional criterion, you must also select the And or Or option to indicate the logical relationship between the criteria.

Figure 4-3   How to perform a simple query (part 1 of 2)

Additional information

✓ If you try to return to Excel without creating a query, Query displays a dialog box that says your query doesn't contain any data. Then, you can end Query without returning any data to Excel or you can remain in Query.

✓ To return to Excel without returning the selected data, click on the Cancel button in the Get External Data dialog box. If you try to switch to Excel without exiting from Query, an hourglass icon is displayed on the Excel screen. This icon means that Excel is waiting for the current operation to complete. To complete the operation, switch back to Query and issue the Return Data command to exit from the program.

✓ If you select the Keep Query Definition option in the Get External Data dialog box, Excel saves the query definition with the result data in the worksheet. This lets you update the result data or edit the query later without entering the specifications for the query again.

✓ If you select the Include Field Names option in the Get External Data dialog box, Excel includes the field names from the database as column labels in the first row of the result data. In other words, the data is formatted as a list.

✓ If you select the Include Row Numbers option in the Get External Data dialog box, Excel includes row numbers as the first column in the list it creates.

4. Click on the Close button, and Query displays the criteria in the criteria pane in the middle of the window and shows the result of the selection in the data pane:

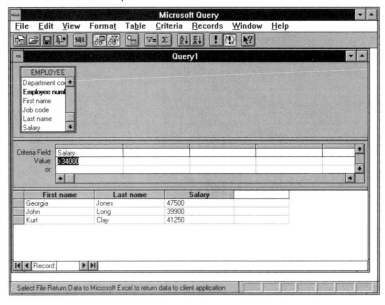

5. Select the Return Data to Microsoft Excel command from the File menu or click on the Return Data button in the toolbar to copy the data to Excel. Then, Excel displays this dialog box:

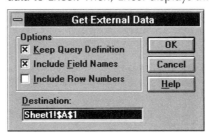

6. Choose the appropriate options, then click on the OK button and the data is inserted in the Excel worksheet in list form:

	A	B	C	D
1	First name	Last name	Salary	
2	Georgia	Jones	47500	
3	John	Long	39900	
4	Kurt	Clay	41250	
5				

Figure 4-3   How to perform a simple query (part 2 of 2)

How to edit a query or update its results

After you retrieve the data from an external database into Excel, you can use the list features presented earlier in this book to work with the data. You can also edit the query that you used to retrieve the data, and you can update the result of the query based on changes made to the external database. Figure 4-4 shows you how to do that.

When you choose to edit a query, you're returned to the Query program where you can select different fields and records from the external database. Then, when you return to Excel, the new data replaces the existing list. When you update the results of a query, Excel works with Query to access the external database and update the data in the existing list. Note that to perform either of these functions, you must save the query definition when you import the data into Excel.

How to work in the Query window

As you select the fields and records you want to include in a query, you'll want to know how to work with the different areas of the Query window. Figure 4-5 presents the basic skills. As you can see, you can manipulate the different areas of the window in several ways to make it easier to work with. In this figure, for example, the tables pane and the Employee field list are enlarged so you can see all of the fields in the list at once.

How to edit a query

1. Place the cell pointer on a cell that contains data from the external database. Then, select the Get External Data command from the Data menu or click on the Get External Data button in the Query and Pivot toolbar. When you do, this dialog box appears:

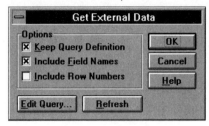

2. Click on the Edit Query button, and you're switched to the Query program.

3. Modify the query. Then, return the data to Excel and the Get External Data dialog box reappears.

4. Change any of the options, then click on the OK button to replace the existing list with the new data.

Three ways to update the results of a query

- Click on the Refresh Data button in the Query and Pivot toolbar.
- Select the Refresh Data command from the Data menu.
- Click on the Refresh button in the Get External Data dialog box.

Notes

- You can edit a query or update its results only if you saved the query definition with the result data. See figure 4-3 for details.
- When you access an external database, the Get External Data button appears in the Query and Pivot toolbar:
- When you update the results of a query, any changes you made to the data in Excel including formatting and sorting are lost.
- You can also switch to the Query program by double-clicking on any cell that contains data from the external database. If you use this technique, however, Excel won't add rows or columns to the data range when you change the query to include additional fields or records. As a result, you may not want to use this technique until it's corrected in a later release of Excel.

Figure 4-4   How to edit a query or update its results

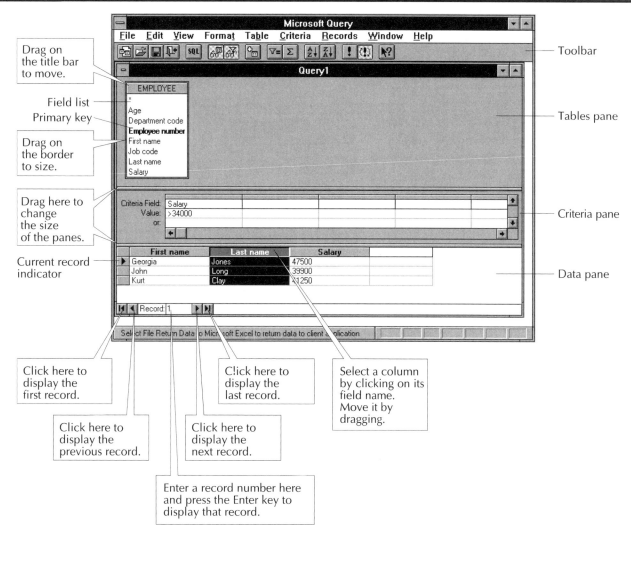

Notes

- The tables pane contains the field list for the database table you selected. If you don't want to see the field list, you can close the tables pane by selecting the Tables command from the View menu or by clicking on the Show/Hide Tables button in the toolbar. See figure 4-6 for a description of the buttons in the toolbar.

- The criteria pane describes the criteria used to select records from the external database. If you don't want to see the criteria, you can close the criteria pane by selecting the Criteria command from the View menu or by clicking on the Show/Hide Criteria button in the toolbar.

- The data pane contains the fields and records you select from the external database. You can scroll through the records in this window using the navigation buttons in the bottom left corner of the pane or the scroll bars that appear when all of the records don't fit in the pane.

Figure 4-5   How to work in the Query window

How to use the Query menus and toolbar buttons

Like other Windows programs, Query lets you issue commands using its menus or the buttons in its toolbar. Figure 4-6 presents the menu commands and toolbar buttons you're most likely to use. Although Query provides commands and buttons for other functions, you're not likely to need those functions when you access Query from Excel. For example, you can use the Save File command in the File menu to save a query in a separate file, but that's not necessary if you save the query with the data that's returned to Excel.

Menu	Command	Function
Table	Remove Table	Removes the selected table from the tables pane.
	Joins	Joins two tables based on the fields you select.
Criteria	Add Criteria	Displays the Add Criteria dialog box so you can specify the criteria for the records you want to retrieve.
	Remove All Criteria	Deletes all of the criteria from the Criteria pane.
Records	Add Column	Displays the Add Column dialog box so you can add another field to the data pane.
	Remove Column	Deletes the selected column from the data pane.
	Sort	Sorts the records in the data pane based on one or more columns you specify.
	Query Now	Performs the query based on the selected fields and records. You'll need to use this command only if you turn the Automatic Query option off.
	Automatic Query	Turns the Automatic Query option on or off. If the database you're accessing contains many records, you may want to turn this option off so the data in the data pane isn't updated every time you change the query. Then, you can use the Query Now command or button to perform the query.

Button	Name	Function
	Return Data	Returns the data to Excel.
	Show/Hide Tables	Opens or closes the tables pane.
	Show/Hide Criteria	Opens or closes the criteria pane.
	Add Table(s)	Displays the Add Tables dialog box so you can select additional tables.
	Criteria Equals	Adds a criterion to the query based on a value that's selected in the data pane.
	Sort Ascending	Sorts the records in the data pane in ascending sequence based on the selected column.
	Sort Descending	Sorts the records in the data pane in descending sequence based on the selected column.
	Query Now	Performs the query based on the selected fields and records.
	Auto Query	Turns the Automatic Query option on or off.
	Help	Displays help for a part of the screen or a selection.

Figure 4-6   **The Query commands and buttons that you're most likely to use**

Exercise set 4-1

1. The following exercises require that you have an external database named Employee. The easiest way to create this file is to save the list you created in chapter 1 as a dBase file. To do that, open the file that contains the list, then highlight the list and select the Save As command to display the Save As dialog box. Next, select one of the DBF formats from the Save File As Type drop-down list, select the directory where you want to store the file, and click on the OK button. When you're done, close the file.

2. Open a new workbook and place the cell pointer on cell A1. Then, use the procedure in figure 4-2 to access the dBase Employee file you created in exercise 1.

3. Use the procedure in figure 4-3 to query the Employee table. The query should include the first name, last name, job code, and salary fields for employees in the Admin department. Import the data into Excel using the default options.

4. Use the technique in the top of figure 4-4 to edit the query created in exercise 3 so that the age field is included and only employees in the Admin department whose salaries are 25,000 or more are selected. Return the data to Excel.

5. Open the file that contains the Employee list you created in chapter 1. Change the salary for Edward Johnson from 33,250 to 35,000, then use the Save As command as described in exercise 1 to save the modified list in the same dBase file you created in that exercise. Switch back to the worksheet that contains the data extracted from the dBase file, and use one of the techniques in figure 4-4 to update the results of the query. Notice that the change you made to the Employee database is reflected in the query results.

6. Switch to the Query program, then use the techniques in figure 4-5 to size the field list so that all of the fields are displayed. To do that, you'll have to increase the size of the tables pane. Then, resequence the fields in the data pane so the column that contains job codes comes after the column that contains salaries. If the criteria pane is closed, click on the Show/Hide Criteria button in the Query toolbar to display it.

Other ways to create a query

Earlier in this chapter, you learned some of the techniques for selecting the fields and records for a query. But Query provides other ways for selecting fields and records that you may want to know about. You'll learn those techniques now. In addition, you'll learn how to edit and delete criteria you've already specified.

How to select fields

Figure 4-7 shows you several ways to select fields from an external database. You already know the first technique for selecting a field from the field list, but you can also select two or more fields or all the fields using the field list. These techniques are presented in the top part of figure 4-7.

Although using the field list is the easiest way to select fields, you can also select fields using the blank column in the data pane. This column is always located to the right of the last column in the data pane. To add a field, select it from the drop-down list that's displayed when you click on the arrow in the heading box at the top of the column, or enter the field name directly into the heading box.

How to select fields using the field list in the tables pane

- To select a single field, double-click on the field in the field list, or drag it from the field list to the data pane. If you drag the field, it's inserted to the left of the column where you drag it.

- To select two or more fields, hold down the Ctrl key as you click on each field in the field list. Or, to select a range of fields, click on the first field, then hold down the Ctrl key and click on the last field. After you select the fields, drag them to the data pane.

- To select all the fields in the field list and add them to the data pane in the order they were created in the external database, double-click on the asterisk (*) at the beginning of the field list. To add all the fields in alphabetical order, double-click on the title bar of the field list. Then, drag the fields to the data pane.

How to select fields using the blank column in the data pane

- Click in the heading box of the blank column to display the drop-down arrow. Then, click on the arrow to display a list of the fields in the table:

First name	Last name	Salary
Mary	Smith	Age
Georgia	Jones	Department code
John	Long	Employee number
Edward	Johnson	First name
John	Jones	Job code
Alice	Williams	Last name
Joel	Allen	Salary
Kurt	Clay	
Patricia	Burkes	
Anne	Andrews	
Barry	Russell	
John	Thompson	

Select a field name from the list.

- Type a field name into the heading box of the blank column, and press the Enter key.

Figure 4-7   How to select fields from an external database (part 1 of 2)

The last technique for selecting fields is using the Add Column command. Unless you want to change the column heading Query uses for the field, though, there's really no reason to use this command.

How to select fields using the Add Column command

- Select the Add Column command from the Records menu, and this dialog box appears:

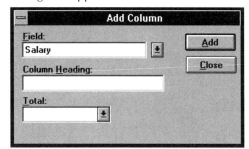

Select a field name from the Field drop-down list, or type a field name into the Field text box. Then, click on the Add button.

How to remove selected fields

- Click on the field name in the data pane to select the column, or drag the mouse over the field names to select two or more columns. Then, press the Delete key or select the Remove Column command from the Records menu.

Note

- As you select fields, Query displays the field names, along with the values for those fields for every record in the database, in the data pane. If you want to display only the field names and not the data, select the Automatic Query command from the Records menu or click on the Auto Query button in the toolbar to turn the Automatic Query option off. Then, you can display the data for the selected fields at any time by selecting the Query Now command from the Records menu or by clicking on the Query Now button in the toolbar.

Additional information

✓ You can also edit the field in a column. To do that, double-click on the field name in the data pane, or select the column and choose the Edit Column command from the Records menu. Then, Query displays a dialog box that lets you select another field or change the name that's displayed for the field in the data pane.

Figure 4-7   How to select fields from an external database (part 2 of 2)

How to select records

Earlier in this chapter, you learned how to select records for a query using the Add Criteria command. Figure 4-8 expands on what you learned. Notice that instead of typing a comparison value into the Value text box, you can click on the Values button and select a value from all of those that occur in the database.

Additional information

✓ By default, the criteria pane is displayed the first time you specify criteria for a query. If it's not displayed, click on the Hide/Show Criteria button in the toolbar or select the Criteria command from the View menu to display it.

✓ If the Automatic Query option is not selected, the results of the criteria you specify aren't reflected in the data pane until you click on the Query Now button in the toolbar or select the Query Now command from the Records menu. To select the Automatic Query option and update the records in the data pane automatically, click on the Auto Query button in the toolbar or select the Automatic Query command from the Records menu.

Access   **Menu**   Criteria ➡ Add Criteria

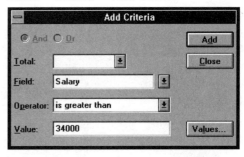

Procedure

1. Access the Add Criteria dialog box.

2. Select the field you want to base the comparison on from the Field drop-down list.

3. Select a relational operator for the comparison from the Operator drop-down list.

4. Enter a comparison value in the Value text box, or click on the Values button to display this dialog box:

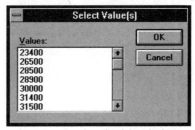

Select a value by double-clicking on it or by highlighting it and clicking on the OK button. This returns you to the Add Criteria dialog box.

5. Click on the Add button to accept the criteria.

6. To specify additional criteria, select the And or Or option to indicate the logical relationship between the criteria. Then, repeat steps 2 through 5.

7. Click on the Close button to close the dialog box.

Notes

• You can use the Total text box in the Add Criteria dialog box to select records based on a calculated field. See the online Help for Query for more information on calculated fields.

• The list that's displayed in the Select Value(s) dialog box includes all the values for the comparison field that occur in the database.

Figure 4-8   How to select records using the Add Criteria command

In most cases, you'll use the Add Criteria command to select the records you want. However, if you want to select all the records that are equal to a value in the database, you can also use the Criteria Equals button. Figure 4-9 shows you how to use this button. Note that if you use this button to specify two or more criteria, Query determines the logical operator automatically. The operator it chooses depends on whether you're adding a criterion to a column or specifying a criterion for a new column.

Procedure

1. Click in a cell in the data pane that contains the value you want to use for the criterion, and the value is highlighted:

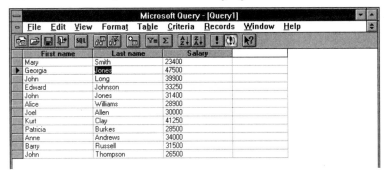

2. Click on the Criteria Equals button in the toolbar. The criteria is displayed in the criteria pane, and the data pane is updated so that it displays only those records that meet the criteria:

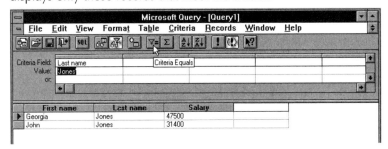

3. Repeat steps 1 and 2 to specify additional criteria.

Note

- If you add a criterion for a field for which you've already specified other criteria, Query adds the new criterion using the Or logical operator. If no other criteria have been specified for a field, Query uses the And logical operator. If you specify multiple criteria, you'll want to experiment with this to see how it works.

Figure 4-9   How to select records using the Criteria Equals button

How to edit and delete criteria

If the query you perform doesn't produce the results you want, you may want to edit or delete the criteria that are used to select the records. Figure 4-10 shows how to do that. When you edit the criteria, you can edit the field the criteria is based on, or you can edit the condition for the field as illustrated in the figure. In most cases, it's easiest just to edit the criteria directly in the criteria pane rather than working through the dialog boxes.

Two ways to change the criteria field

- Click in the cell that contains the name of the field you want to change, and a drop-down arrow appears. Click on the drop-down arrow and select another field from the list that's displayed.

- Double-click in the cell that contains the name of the field you want to change, and this dialog box appears:

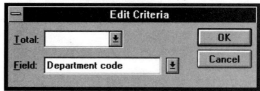

Click on the drop-down arrow to the right of the Field text box and select a field from the list that's displayed.

Two ways to change the condition for a field

- Click in the cell that contains the condition you want to change and enter the new condition.

- Double-click in the cell that contains the condition you want to change and this dialog box appears:

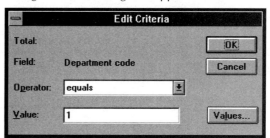

Select a new operator from the drop-down list. Then, enter a new value in the Value text box, or click on the Values button and select a value from the list that's displayed.

How to delete criteria

- To delete all of the criteria, select the Remove All Criteria command from the Criteria menu.

- To delete the criteria for a single field, position the mouse pointer at the top of the column in the criteria pane so that it turns into a down arrow. Click to select the column, then press the Delete key.

Figure 4-10   How to edit and delete criteria

Exercise set 4-2

1. Use the technique in figure 4-7 to remove all of the selected fields from the data pane. Then, use the techniques in figure 4-7 to select all of the fields except the department field.

2. Delete all the criteria in the criteria pane by selecting the Remove All Criteria command from the Criteria menu. Then, use the Add Criteria and Select Value(s) dialog boxes as described in figure 4-8 to select records for employees who are 30 or older.

3. Use the Criteria Equals button as described in figure 4-9 to select records for employees with job code 3.

4. Use the techniques in figure 4-10 to change the criteria so that only the records for employees in the Admin department are selected.

Other skills for using Microsoft Query

The skills presented so far in this chapter are the ones you need to know to perform most queries. However, there are some additional skills you might need to use from time to time. You'll learn three of those skills next. First, you'll learn how to sort the data in the data pane. Second, you'll learn how to create a query using fields from two or more tables. Third, you'll learn how to enable the Query add-in program if it isn't available from the Excel menu.

How to sort the records in the data pane

Figure 4-11 shows you how to sort the data in the data pane. If you want to sort on a single column, you can use the Sort Ascending and Sort Descending buttons in the toolbar. If you want to sort on one or more columns, you can use the Sort command. You can also use the Sort command to remove one or more sort specifications.

As you know, you can also sort the records once they're returned to Query. If you update the results of the Query, however, the sort is lost. On the other hand, the sort is maintained if it's done in Query. If you update frequently, then, and you want to maintain the records in a specific sort sequence, sorting the records in Query makes sense.

Additional information

✓ When you use the toolbar buttons for sorting, the sort you specify replaces any previous sort. To sort by more than one column, use the Sort command.

✓ When you delete a sort specification, the records are returned to the sequence in which they appeared before they were sorted.

How to sort using the toolbar buttons

1. Select the field you want to sort on by clicking on the field name at the top of the column:

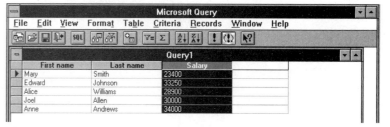

2. Click on the Sort Ascending or Sort Descending button in the toolbar, and the records are sorted:

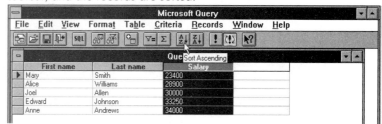

How to sort using the Sort command

1. Select the Sort command from the Records menu and this dialog box appears:

2. Select the column you want to sort on, select the Ascending or Descending option, and click on the Add button. The sort specification is added to the Sorts in Query list box and the records are sorted.

3. Repeat step 2 for each column you want to sort on.

4. Click on the Close button to close the dialog box.

How to delete a sort specification

1. Select the Sort command from the Records menu to display the Sort dialog box.

2. Highlight the sort specification in the Sorts In Query list box and click on the Remove button.

Figure 4-11   How to sort the records in the data pane

How to create a query using fields from two or more tables

The queries you've seen up to this point have retrieved data from a single table. In some cases, however, the information you want may be stored in two or more tables. To retrieve data from more than one table, you use the techniques presented in figure 4-12.

To begin, you add all of the tables you want to access to the tables pane. If the tables are related by primary key fields, Query *joins* the tables automatically. The join lines in the tables pane indicate how the tables are joined. In figure 4-12, for example, the Department and Job tables are joined by the Department code field. And the Job and Employee tables are joined by the Department code and Job code fields. When the tables are joined like this, you can select fields and records from the tables using the same techniques you use with a single table.

A query that accesses data from three tables

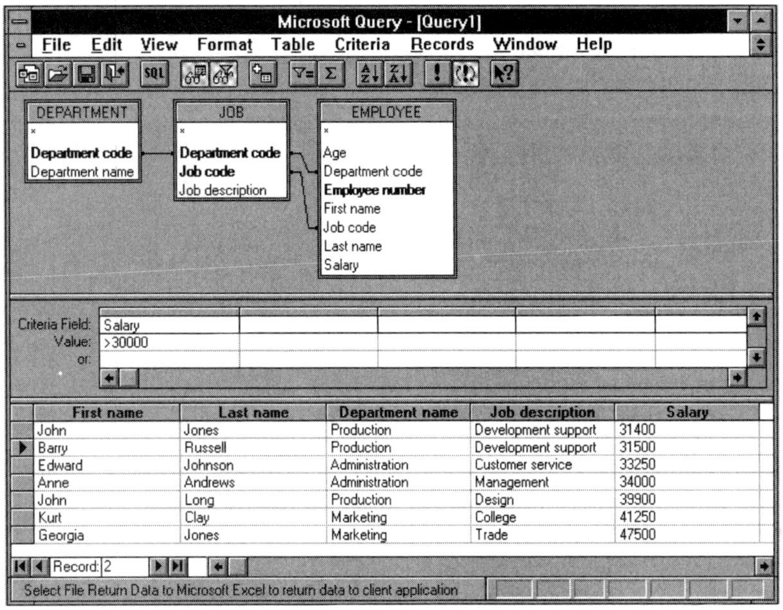

Operation

- To add a table to a query, select the Add Tables command from the Table menu or click on the Add Tables button in the toolbar to display the Add Tables dialog box. Select the table you want to add, then close the dialog box. If the table has a field with the same name and data type as the field in another table in the query and the field is a primary key in one of the tables, Query joins the two tables automatically. The join lines in the tables pane indicate how the tables are joined.

- To remove a table from a query, click in the field list for the table, then select the Remove Table command from the Table menu.

- To select fields from the tables, use the techniques presented in figure 4-7.

- To select records from the tables, use the techniques presented in figures 4-8 and 4-9.

Notes

- If the external database program doesn't support primary key fields, you have to define the joins yourself. See figure 4-13 for details.

- When Query joins tables automatically, it creates an *equi-join*. With this type of join, records are selected only if the joined fields are equal. To create a different type of join, use the Joins dialog box presented in figure 4-13.

Figure 4-12   How to create a query using fields from two or more tables

If the tables you choose aren't related by primary key fields, you'll want to create the joins before you select fields and records. To do that, you use one of the techniques in figure 4-13. The easiest way to join two tables is by using the mouse to drag a field in one table to a field in the other table. When you create a join using this technique, Query creates an *equi-join*. That means that a record is selected only if the joined fields are equal. This is the type of join you'll use most often, and it's the type of join Query creates automatically when you use tables that are related by key fields.

To create a join other than an equi-join, you use the Joins command as illustrated in figure 4-13. When you use this command, you can select an operator other than "equals" to define the join, and you can select an option that determines what records are included in the query. You can also use the Joins command to delete a join.

Additional information

✓ When you work with two or more tables, Query prefixes the field names with the name of the table. That way, you can distinguish between fields with the same name in different tables.

✓ If you select the first option from the Join Includes group of the Joins dialog box, only those records whose joined fields match are included. If you select the second or third option, all of the records in one of the tables are included. Then, the data from the records in the other table is included only if the joined fields in the two records match. You can't use this type of join if there are more than two tables in the query.

How to create a join using the mouse

- Drag the field you want to join in one table to the field you want to join it with in another table. Query joins the two fields using an equi-join.

How to create a join using the Joins command

1. Select the Joins command from the Table menu and this dialog box appears:

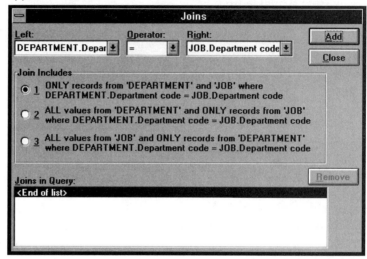

2. Click on the drop-down arrow to the right of the Left text box, and select the field in the first table you want to join from the drop-down list that's displayed.

3. Click on the drop-down arrow to the right of the Operator text box, and select the operator you want to use to join the two fields from the drop-down list that's displayed. In most cases, you'll use the equals operator (=), which is the default.

4. Click on the drop-down arrow to the right of the Right text box, and select the field in the second table you want to join from the drop-down list that's displayed.

5. Select an option from the Join Includes group. The option you select determines what records are included in the query.

6. Click on the Add button to create the join.

7. Repeat steps 2 through 6 to create additional joins.

8. Click on the Close button to close the dialog box.

Two ways to delete a join

- Click on the join line in the tables pane to select it, then press the Delete key.

- Access the Joins dialog box by selecting the Joins command from the Table menu or by double-clicking on the join line. Highlight the join in the Joins In Query list box and click on the Remove button.

Figure 4-13   How to join two tables

How to enable the Query add-in program

Figure 4-14 shows you how to enable the Query add-in program. If you installed Query when you installed Excel, Query is enabled by default. That means that when you start Excel, the Get External Data command is available from the Data menu. If you didn't install Query when you installed Excel, you'll need to install it before you can enable it from Excel. The second note in figure 4-14 summarizes the procedure for installing Query.

Access   **Menu**   Tools ➡ Add-ins

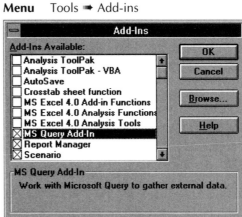

Operation

• To enable the Query add-in program so it's available when you start Excel, select the MS Query Add-in option from the Add-Ins Available list box.

Notes

• The add-ins that appear in the Add-Ins Available list box are those that were set up when Excel was installed on your PC. As a result, the Add-Ins dialog box on your PC may look different from the one in this figure.

• If the MS Query Add-in option doesn't appear in the list box, click on the Browse button, then locate and select the file named XLQUERY.XLA. If you can't locate the file, use the Excel Setup program to install it. To do that, start the Setup program from the Excel installation diskettes and click on the Add/Remove button. Select the Data Access option in the dialog box that appears. (The Query add-in program is included in this component and not in the Add-in component.) Do *not* deselect any options that are already selected or they will be removed from your system. If you want to install only the ODBC drivers you need, double-click on the Data Access option or highlight it and click on the Change Option button. Then, deselect the drivers you don't want to install and click on the OK button. Finally, click on the Continue button and Setup will prompt you for the diskettes it needs to install the Data Access components.

Figure 4-14   **How to enable the Query add-in program**

Exercise set 4-3

1. Delete all the criteria from the criteria pane. Then, use the Sort buttons as described in figure 4-11 to sort the records in the data pane in ascending order by salary. Next, use the Sort command as described in figure 4-11 to remove the previous sort and sort the list by age in ascending order within job code in ascending order. Return the data to Excel, then close the workbook without saving the changes.

2. Open a new workbook and create a list that contains the following data:

Job code	Description
1	Support staff
2	Management
3	Executive

   Save the list as a dBase file with the name JOB as described in exercise set 4-1. Close the workbook.

3. Open a new workbook, then use Query to access the Employee and Job dBase files. Use one of the techniques in figure 4-13 to create an equi-join between the Employee and Job tables using their job code fields.

4. Use the techniques you learned throughout this chapter to create a query that includes the first name, last name, and department fields in the Employee table and the job description field in the Job table. The query should include only those records for employees in the Prod department. Return the data to Excel. Then, close the workbook without saving the changes.

Perspective

This chapter presents the Query functions you're most likely to use to import data from an external database into an Excel list. Because Excel makes it easy to manipulate the data in a list, this is a practical and easy way to work with the data in an external database. That's particularly true if you're not familiar with the database program that was used to create the database.

Although Query is packaged with Excel, you can use it from within other programs as well. For example, you can use it with Microsoft Word to extract records from an external database for a mail merge operation. Then, you can use the same techniques you learned in this chapter to select the fields and records you need.

You can also run Query directly from Windows rather than from another program. You may want to do that, for example, if you need to query an external database but you don't need to save the results of the query. When you use Query in this manner, you can use all of the techniques you learned in this chapter. In addition, you may want to use some of the features of Query that aren't presented in this chapter. For example, you can use it to do calculations based on the data it retrieves. You can use it to add, change, and delete records in the external database. And you can use it to save queries you perform regularly. For more information on using Query to perform these functions, refer to the Microsoft Query User's Guide.

Summary

- Query works as an interface between Excel and an external database by retrieving records from the database and returning them to Excel.

- To access Query, use the Get External Data command in the Data menu and identify the database and tables you want to work with.

- To perform a *query*, select the fields you want to include and specify the criteria you want to use to retrieve records. When you return the data to Excel, it's formatted as a list.

- If you save the query definition with the data that's returned to Excel, you can later edit the query to select different fields or records, and you can update the data to reflect changes made to the external database.

- You can select the fields for a query using the field list in the tables pane, the blank column in the data pane, or the Add Column command in the Records menu.

- You can select the records for a query using the Add Criteria command in the Criteria menu or the Criteria Equals button in the toolbar.

- You can edit criteria by changing the criteria field or the condition for the field directly in the criteria pane or by displaying the Edit Criteria dialog box. You can also delete one or more criteria.

- You can sort the records in the data pane using the buttons in the Query toolbar or the Sort command in the Records menu. You can also delete a sort specification using the Sort command.

- You can create a query using the fields in two or more tables. If the tables are related by primary key fields, Query *joins* the tables automatically based on those fields. If the tables aren't related by primary key fields, you must define the joins yourself.

- You can enable the Query program using the Add-Ins command in the Tools menu. If you installed Query when you installed Excel, Query is enabled by default.

Index

A

Accessing an external database, 40-41
Add Column command (Records menu, Query), 46, 49
Add Criteria command (Criteria menu, Query), 42, 46, 50
Add Tables button (Query toolbar), 46, 55
Add Tables command (Table menu, Query), 55
Add-in program, 37
Add-ins command (Tools menu), 57
Adding
    automatic subtotals, 18-19
    pivot table fields, 30
    records using a data form, 9
Advanced Filter feature, 6-8
Asterisk wildcard, 4, 6
Auto Query button (Query toolbar), 46, 49, 50
AutoFill feature, 17
AutoFilter feature, 3-4
Autoformat, 25
Automatic Query command (Records menu, Query), 46, 49, 50
Automatic subtotals, 18-19

B

Browsing records using a data form, 9, 10

C

Case-sensitive sort, 16
Changing
    data formats in a pivot table, 27
    field names in Query, 49
    layout of a pivot table, 26
    names of pivot table fields, 28
    names of summary fields, 27
    normal sort order, 16
    records using a data form, 9
    subtotals in a pivot table, 28
    summary function in a pivot table, 27
Clear Outline command (Group and Outline submenu, Data menu), 19
Column field (pivot table), 24
    adding, 30
    changing the name, 28
    deleting, 28, 30
    moving, 26
Column label, 2
Computed criteria, 6
Creating
    joins, 56
    page fields, 33
    pivot tables, 24-25, 30
    queries using multiple tables, 55-56
    results tables, 8
Criteria, 3, 4
    computed, 6
    deleting from Query, 52
    editing in Query, 52
    entering in data forms, 10
    entering in Query, 42
    removing from data forms, 10

Criteria command (View menu, Query), 45, 50
Criteria Equals button (Query toolbar), 46, 51
Criteria pane (Query window), 42, 45
    displaying, 50
Criteria range, 6, 7, 8
Cue Cards feature (Query), 41
Current record indicator, 45
Custom selection criteria, 3, 4

D

Data field (pivot table), 25
    adding, 30
    deleting, 30
    formatting, 27
Data form, 9-10
Data pane (Query window), 42, 45
    selecting fields, 48
    sorting records, 54
Data range, 15
Database, 38, 39
    accessing, 40-41
    querying, 38
Delete command (Edit menu), 2
Deleting
    column or row fields, 28
    criteria in Query, 52
    fields from a pivot table, 30
    joins, 56
    records using a data form, 9
    sort specifications in Query, 54
Displaying
    criteria pane, 50
    data for selected fields, 50
    hidden rows, 7
    records in the data pane, 45
    results of a query, 50
    source data for a data value, 31
Duplicate records, hiding, 7

E

Edit Column command (Records menu, Query), 49
Editing
    criteria in Query, 52
    fields in Query, 49
    queries, 44
Enabling Query, 57
Entering criteria in a data form, 10
Equi-join, 55, 56
External database, *see Database*

F

Field, 2
    adding to a pivot table, 30
    deleting from a pivot table, 30
    editing in Query, 49
    removing from a query, 49
    selecting in Query, 42, 48

Field list (Query), 45
    selecting fields, 42, 48
Field name, 2
    changing in Query, 49
Filter, 3
Filter command (Data menu), 2
Filtering
    data in a pivot table, 33
    lists using Advanced Filter, 6-7
    lists using AutoFilter, 3-4
    removing from a list, 3, 4
Flat file, 38, 39
Form command (Data menu), 2, 9
Formatting the data in a pivot table, 27

G

Get External Data button (Query and Pivot toolbar), 44
Get External Data command (Data menu), 40, 44, 57
Grand totals (pivot table), 25, 28
Group button (Query and Pivot toolbar), 23, 32
Group command (Group and Outline submenu, Data menu), 32
Grouping numeric items, 32

H

Header row, 2
Help button (Query toolbar), 46
Hidden rows, displaying, 7
Hide Detail button (Query and Pivot toolbar), 23, 31
Hide Detail command (Group and Outline submenu,
        Data menu), 19, 31
Hide/Show Criteria button (Query toolbar), 50
Hiding
    data in a pivot table, 31
    duplicate records, 7
    information in an outline, 19
    pivot table items, 28
    subtotals in a pivot table, 28

I

Installing Query, 57

J

Join, 56
Joining tables, 55-56
Joins command (Table menu, Query), 46, 56

L

List, 1
    adding automatic subtotals, 18-19
    filtering, 3-4, 6-7
    setting up, 2
    sorting, 15-17
Logical operators, 4

M

Microsoft Query, *see Query program*
Moving
    column fields, 26
    field lists, 45
    pivot table items, 26
    row fields, 26

N

Non-relational database, 38, 39
    accessing, 41
Normal sort order, 16
Numeric items, grouping, 32

O

Open database connectivity (ODBC) driver, 37, 39
Operators, 4
Outline feature, 19

P

Page field (pivot table), 33
Pivot table, 22
    adding fields, 30
    changing, 26-28
    creating, 24-25, 30
    deleting fields, 30
    filtering, 33
    grouping numeric items, 32
    hiding and showing data, 31
    saving the source data, 25
    updating the contents, 29
Pivot table item, 25
    hiding, 28
    hiding or showing subordinates, 31
    moving, 26
    removing, 28
PivotTable command (Data menu), 24
PivotTable Field button (Query and Pivot toolbar), 23, 27, 28
PivotTable Field command (Data menu), 27, 28
PivotTable Wizard, 24-25, 26, 27, 29, 30, 33
    accessing Query, 41
PivotTable Wizard button (Query and Pivot toolbar), 23
Primary key, 45
Primary key field, 55
Primary sort key, 15

Q

Query
    editing, 44
    saving with the result data, 43
Query and Pivot toolbar, 23
Query interface, 38
Query menus, 46
Query Now button (Query toolbar), 46, 49, 50
Query Now command (Records menu, Query), 46, 49, 50
Query program, 37, 39
    accessing an external database, 40-41
    editing criteria, 52
    enabling, 57
    joining tables, 55-56
    removing fields, 49
    selecting fields, 42, 48-49, 50-51
    selecting records, 42, 50-51
    sorting data, 54
Query results
    displaying, 50
    updating, 44
Query table, 8
Query toolbar, 45, 46
Query window, 44, 45
Querying a database, 38, 42-43
Question mark wildcard, 4, 6

R

Records, 2
    selecting in Query, 42, 50-51
    selecting using AutoFilter, 3-4
    working with in a data form, 10
Refresh Data button (Query and Pivot toolbar), 23, 29, 44
Refresh Data command (Data menu), 29, 44
Relational database, 38, 39
    accessing, 40-41
Relational operators, 4
Remove All Criteria command (Criteria menu, Query), 46, 52
Remove Column command (Records menu, Query), 46, 49
Remove Table command (Table menu, Query), 46, 55
Removing
    automatic subtotals from a list, 18, 19
    criteria from a data form, 10
    fields from a query, 49
    filtering from a list, 3, 4
    outlines, 19
    pivot table items, 28
Results table, 6
    creating, 8
Retaining the unsorted sequence, 17
Return Data button (Query toolbar), 43, 46
Return Data to Microsoft Excel command (File menu, Query), 43
Row field (pivot table), 24
    adding, 30
    changing the name, 28
    deleting, 28, 30
    moving, 26
Rows command (Insert menu), 2

S

Save File command (File menu, Query), 46
Saving
    query definitions with the result data, 43
    source data with a pivot table, 25
Secondary sort key, 15
Selecting
    columns in the data pane, 45
    fields in Query, 42, 48-49
Selecting records from a list
    Advanced Filter feature, 7
    AutoFilter feature, 3-4
    data forms, 10
Selecting records in Query, 42, 50-51
Selection criteria
    custom, 3, 4
    entering in Query, 42
Setting up
    criteria ranges, 6
    lists, 2
Setup program, 57
Show All command (Filter submenu, Data menu), 4, 7
Show Detail button (Query and Pivot toolbar), 23, 31
Show Detail command (Group and Outline submenu, Data menu), 19, 31
Show Pages button (Query and Pivot toolbar), 23
Show/Hide Criteria button (Query toolbar), 45, 46
Show/Hide Tables button (Query toolbar), 45, 46

Showing
    data in pivot tables, 31
    information in outlines, 19
Sizing
    field lists, 45
    panes in the Query window, 45
Sort Ascending button
    Query toolbar, 46, 54
    Standard toolbar, 17
Sort command
    Data menu, 15
    Records menu (Query), 46, 54
Sort Descending button
    Query toolbar, 46, 54
    Standard toolbar, 17
Sort key, 15
Sort order, 16
Sort specification, deleting, 54
Sorting
    lists, 15-17
    records in the data pane, 54
Source data, displaying, 31
Subtotals
    automatic, 18-19
    changing in pivot tables, 28
    hiding, 28
    pivot tables, 25
Subtotals command (Data menu), 18
Summary field, 27
Summary function (pivot table), 25
    changing, 27

T

Tables (database), 38
    joining, 55-56
Tables command (View menu, Query), 45
Tables pane (Query window), 40, 45
Text wrapping, 2
Toolbars command (View menu), 23

U

Ungroup button (Query and Pivot toolbar), 23, 32
Ungroup command (Group and Outline submenu, Data menu), 32
Ungrouping numeric items, 32
Unsorted sequence, 17
Updating
    pivot table contents, 29
    query results, 44

W

Wildcard characters, 4, 6
Wrapping text, 2

"This book includes virtually anything that anybody wants to know about this most versatile spreadsheet program....."

–Jerry Haberkost, PC Users Group of South Jersey

The Essential Guide: Excel 5 for Windows

by Anne Prince

Here are just some of the features you'll find:

- Working with multiple worksheets
- Printing skills
- Charting
- Graphics
- Auditing a worksheet
- Using macros
- OLE
- Scenario Manager
- The Goal Seek and Solver commands

Excel 5 for Windows offers so many features, it's impossible to remember all the details of using each one. What's more, unless you've had plenty of time to experiment with the program, you probably aren't even aware of some of the features that could help you out the most.

That's why you need a quick, comprehensive reference to Excel. And Anne Prince has written one: *The Essential Guide to Excel 5 for Windows*. Anne's divided the content up into 24 task-oriented chapters in 5 sections, with subheads that make it easy for you to quickly find what you're looking. And like this book on Excel lists, *The Essential Guide* is heavily illustrated, with all the information in the figures. So you can often start using a new feature without even reading the text. And you can look up forgotten details about any feature in just a moment or two.

24 chapters, 497 pages, 295 illustrations, **$25.00**
ISBN 0-911625-79-8

For newcomers to Excel 5 who want to learn how to use the program most efficiently right from the start...

Work Like a Pro with Excel 5 for Windows

by Anne Prince

Contents

Section 1
Get started right with Excel 5
How to create, print, and save a worksheet
How to edit and format a worksheet
Commands and features for working with larger worksheets

Section 2
The features that help you work like a pro
Commands and features that improve your productivity
How to work with more than one worksheet in a single file
How to create charts and graphs
How to set Excel up so it works the way you want it to

The trouble with most PC books, manuals, help facilities, and courses is that it takes too long to get the information you need. As a result, you stick to the skills you already have, even though you know there must be a better way. That's why all too many people use Excel 5 as if it were one of the early releases of Lotus 1-2-3. They just don't have time to learn the current timesaving features that can help them work more productively.

To combat this problem, Anne Prince has written an introductory book called *Work Like a Pro with Excel 5 for Windows*. It presents all the critical skills that most professionals need...with none of the irrelevant details that distract and confuse. It emphasizes concepts by presenting generalized procedures that you can use with any data instead of step-by-step procedures that are limited to specific data. And it's set up just like this book, relying more on visual presentation than on text.

So if someone you know needs to learn Excel 5, get them off to a great start by recommending *Work Like a Pro with Excel 5 for Windows*.

7 chapters, approx. 224 pages, **$20.00**
ISBN 0-911625-89-5

Available May 1995

Order/Comment Form

Your opinions count

If you have any comments, criticisms, or suggestions for us, I'm eager to get them. Your opinions today will affect our products of tomorrow. And if you find any errors in this book, typographical or otherwise, please point them out so we can correct them in the next printing. Thanks for your help.

Book title:

Excel 5 for Windows: How to work with lists, pivot tables, and external databases

Dear Mike:

_____
_____
_____
_____
_____
_____
_____
_____
_____
_____
_____
_____

Our Ironclad Guarantee
To our customers who order directly from us: You must be satisfied. Our books must work for you, or you can send them back for a full refund...no questions asked.

To order more quickly,

Call toll-free 1-800-221-5528
(Weekdays, 8 to 5 Pacific Time)
Fax: 1-209-275-9035

Mike Murach & Associates, Inc.
4697 West Jacquelyn Avenue
Fresno, California 93722-6427
(209) 275-3335

Name (& Title, if any) _____

Company (if company address) _____

Street address _____

City, State, Zip _____

Phone number (including area code) _____

Fax number (if you fax your order to us) _____

Qty	Product code and title	*Price
_____	LWIN **The Least You Need to Know about Windows 3.1**	$20.00
_____	EXLS **Excel 5: How to work with lists, pivot tables, & external databases**	11.95
_____	PREX **Work Like a Pro with Excel 5 (available May 1995)**	20.00
_____	EEX5 **The Essential Guide: Excel 5 for Windows**	25.00
_____	MWMM **Word 6: How to use the Mail Merge feature**	9.95
_____	PRMW **Work Like a Pro with Word 6 (available May 1995)**	20.00
_____	MWW6 **The Essential Guide: Word 6 for Windows**	25.00
_____	WPW6 **The Essential Guide: WordPerfect 6 for Windows**	25.00
_____	ELW4 **The Essential Guide: 1-2-3 for Windows Release 4**	20.00

☐ Bill me for the books plus UPS shipping and handling (and sales tax within CA).

☐ Bill my company. P.O.#_____

☐ I want to **SAVE 10%** by paying in advance.
Charge to my ____Visa ____MasterCard ____American Express:

Card number _____

Valid thru (mo/yr) _____

Cardowner's signature _____

☐ I want to **SAVE 10% plus shipping and handling**. Here's my check for the books minus 10% ($_____). California residents, please add sales tax to your total. (Offer valid in U.S.)

*Prices are subject to change. Please call for current prices.

BUSINESS REPLY MAIL

FIRST-CLASS MAIL   PERMIT NO. 3063   FRESNO, CA

POSTAGE WILL BE PAID BY ADDRESSEE

Mike Murach & Associates, Inc.

4697 W JACQUELYN AVE
FRESNO CA 93722-9888